Research-Based Strategies
for English Language Learners

*We dedicate this book to all the teachers who have practiced
these scaffolds with ELL students, found them effective,
and then shared their stories. We share with you a dream for
all English language learners to be treated with respect
and achieve to their highest potential.*

—Denise Rea and Sandra Mercuri

*I also dedicate this book to my husband Freddy.
Without his encouragement and support this
book would have not been possible.*

—Sandra Mercuri

Research-Based Strategies for English Language Learners

How to Reach Goals and Meet Standards, K–8

Denise M. Rea

Sandra P. Mercuri

HEINEMANN
Portsmouth, NH

Heinemann

361 Hanover Street
Portsmouth, NH 03801–3912
www.heinemann.com

Offices and agents throughout the world

Library of Congress Cataloging-in-Publication Data
Rea, Denise M.
    Research-based strategies for English language learners : how to reach goals and meet standards, K–8 / Denise M. Rea, Sandra P. Mercuri ; foreword by Yvonne S. Freeman and David E. Freeman.
        p. cm.
    Includes bibliographical references and index.
    ISBN-13: 978-0-325-00810-3
    ISBN-10: 0-325-00810-8
    1. Language arts (Elementary).   2. English language—Study and teaching.   3. English language—Study and teaching—Foreign speakers.   4. Language experience approach in education.   I. Mercuri, Sandra.   II. Title.
LB1576.R392   2006
372.6—dc22   2006019540

Editor: Lois Bridges
Production service: Kim Arney
Production coordination: Vicki Kasabian
Cover design: Night and Day Design
Typesetter: Kim Arney
Manufacturing: Steve Bernier

Printed in the United States of America on acid-free paper
21 20 19 18   VP   10 11 12 13

Contents

Acknowledgments

During our years as teachers in the Central Valley of California, we continually tried to improve our instruction to meet the needs of the highly ELL populated schools in which we worked. We were challenged but also thrived as we learned with and from our students.

In our years as teacher educators at Fresno Pacific, we have had the privilege of working with many outstanding teachers who draw on the rich diversity in their classrooms to create exemplary learning communities in which English language learners find success.

While this book mainly tells of our own experiences in the classroom working with second language learners, it also has been shaped by our conversations with master teachers, our observations of student teachers with amazing talent to put theory into practice, and by the lessons shared by some teachers in this area and across the country.

We would especially like to acknowledge Drs. Yvonne and David Freeman, who encouraged us to write this book. They believed that our ideas would be valuable for many teachers working with English learners who are struggling to provide the best education possible for their students.

We also want to acknowledge the student teachers with whom we worked at our university. Through them we re-lived the challenges that many teachers face in schools today, and we learned from their strengths.

We want to thank Mr. Elliott and his sixth-grade class from the Salt Lake City School District for sharing with us the mural picture that we used in chapter five to accompany the lesson, as well as Becky Stiglich, the student teacher who shared with us the project about *Romeo and Juliet* used in chapter six. These contributions also helped us show how scaffolds work across grade levels and content areas.

Finally we would like to thank our editor, Lois Bridges. While she is no longer with Heinemann, she has helped us revise and better conceptualize our ideas through her thoughtful suggestions and comments.

Foreword

During the sixteen years we taught and wrote in Fresno, California, we had the opportunity to meet and work with many talented teachers. Two of the most talented were Denise Rea and Sandra Mercuri. Both were students in our master's degree program, which prepared teachers to work with bilingual students. Denise and Sandra both had the special gift of taking theory and research and putting it into practice, the topic of this book.

Since completing their master's degrees, Denise and Sandra have had many additional important experiences that have added to the richness of this book. Denise has served as a specialist for working effectively with second language students in her large and diverse school district and, because of her own research and writing, she was designated the Hmong language and culture specialist. This designation proved her dedication to the large numbers of Hmong students who were not being well served in her area. Because of her expertise and the large numbers of ELL students in area classrooms, Denise was asked by a local university to work part-time as a supervisor of student teachers. This position led to a full-time university position, and she presently serves as the Teacher Education Director, planning curriculum for all future teachers who will need to be prepared for the diverse students who will be in their classrooms.

Sandra is an immigrant. She and her family came to this country ten years ago. Sandra's experiences were not the same as those of many children in our schools because she came to this country well prepared academically and with some English. However, that does not mean that Sandra and her family did not face many challenges. Her experiences adjusting to a new country and new culture have helped Sandra understand the struggles that second language learners face. In order to get a teaching credential, Sandra had to take coursework and standardized tests in a language and within a cultural context that were new to her. While taking university coursework, Sandra worked as an intern teacher of migrant students. She quickly realized that traditional teaching was not effective with her newcomer students. When she read the research and studied effective practices for bilingual students, she decided to put research and theory into practice. She was so successful with this that she was nominated as an outstanding teacher in her district. Sandra began to share her successes in teaching at conferences and was asked, because of her strong teaching and her bilingualism, to direct a grant for dual language teacher preparation at a local university. Sandra now teaches full-time at the university and counsels teachers working on an M.A. degree in both TESOL and bilingual education. In addition, she is completing a doctoral degree at the University of California at Davis.

It is important for readers to understand the strong academic and experiential backgrounds that these two teachers bring to this book. The ideas that Denise and Sandra share here are tried and true. These two authors wrote this book because they believed there were not enough practical ideas laid out for teachers working with ELL students. It is their hope that this book will fill a gap and help teachers, even those in the present climate of testing and overemphasis on skills instruction, to meet the academic needs of their diverse students.

Research-Based Strategies for English Language Learners blends theory and practice. Each chapter provides the research base for the strategies that are introduced. The strategies are carefully described. Scenarios from a variety of classrooms help bring the strategies to life. One especially helpful feature is a summary section at the end of Chapters 2 through 5 called *The Chapter in a Nutshell*. These pages provide a clear summary of the strategies described in the chapter. The authors have extensive background working in classrooms with English language learners. They also have studied the research that supports effective practice for second language students. In this book they share their experiences by providing many practical, research-based strategies that teachers can immediately put into practice.

—Yvonne S. Freeman and David E. Freeman

Introduction

I have been in classrooms where students don't speak any English. They don't understand what is being said and seem totally lost. There is no special instruction for them. I saw one student just put his head down on the desk and cry. The teacher just ignored him. Is this the right thing to do?

— DEBBIE, PRESERVICE TEACHER

Debbie's question—"Is this the right thing to do?"—is the motivation for this book. How can teachers provide challenging and engaging instruction in academically, linguistically, racially, ethnically, and socially diverse classrooms? How do English language learners learn to speak English well? How can all students succeed in a rigorous curriculum in which no one is left behind?

Every year there are more and more English language learners in our schools. Students with cultural and linguistic differences are now or soon will be the norm rather than the exception in mainstream classrooms. Since 1998, the number of students not fluent in English has almost doubled, while the student population as a whole has remained essentially the same. In California, for example:

- More than 60 percent of students are students of color.
- 80 percent of teachers are Caucasian.
- 40 percent of students are Latino.
- One out of four children is learning English as a second language.
- About one out of three children enters kindergarten speaking a language other than English. (California State Department of Education 1996)

The reality is this: the new mainstream classroom comprises both English language learners and native speakers of English.

Some English language learners arrive with adequate schooling in their primary language. These students usually catch up academically. Others arrive with limited or no schooling in their primary language. These students are below grade level in all areas and generally struggle throughout their schooling. The most forgotten subgroup of English language learners are the long-term English language learners. These students have been in the U.S. school system for at least seven years. They have been able to develop only conversational English language skills and are struggling in all areas of literacy. Many times their teachers assume they have not only conversational speaking skills but academic English skills as well. Generally they do not. They often come from low socioeconomic backgrounds and homes in which literacy is minimal. The interventions and instruction they have received have been inadequate, and they are highly likely to drop out before they graduate from high school (Freeman, Freeman, and Mercuri 2002).

While the native speakers of English are fluent conversationalists, they may still need to develop language skills in English. They come with diverse needs, abilities, strengths, experiences, and interests. They may come from low socioeconomic backgrounds and homes in which literacy is little valued. (There is a growing trend to include students with learning disabilities in the mainstream classroom as well.)

Teachers know they are not reaching some of these students. Traditional teaching, with rows of desks occupied by isolated students completing worksheets and answering textbook questions, is no longer adequate. Attendance is too irregular, there are too many disruptions, and there is a huge span of reading abilities. Students come with background experiences, values, and knowledge unique to their cultural ethnicities, and classes include learners with many different first languages at various stages of English language acquisition.

In his research on effective teachers, William Sanders says that the single greatest effect on student performance is the teacher. It's not race or poverty as many people believe. (Sanders 1996). What teachers do matters. This book asks teachers to use all the tools in their toolbox, to take their best practices and synthesize them with valuable new scaffolds so that all students' instructional needs and learning styles are addressed and all students have the opportunity to perform to their potential.

What Are Instructional Scaffolds?

Scaffolds are common in the construction industry, but the term is also a useful metaphor when applied to teaching. In the classroom, a teacher uses a scaffold to support a student's understanding of a concept or skill. A scaffold has been described as a deliberate course of action that teachers create to help students focus on ideas and processes (McKenzie 2000). While essential, a scaffold is temporary and is withdrawn when students no longer need the support. The scaffolds presented in this book are based on practices that have been identified in the literature as essential for supporting the academic progress of English language learners. These strategies can be used in any curricular area (this book includes examples drawn from social studies and science) and almost any grade level, K–8. Remember too that a scaffold is not used in isolation and that two or more can be used in a given lesson. The teacher uses experience and expertise to blend scaffolds to suit the interests and abilities of the students.

Teachers may already use scaffolds and not know it. A scaffold can be as simple as asking students to draw pictures of the beginning, middle, and end of a story before writing or arranging students into heterogeneous ability groups to work on a project. Scaffolds offer many benefits.

- They clarify the purpose of a lesson for English language learners.
- Scaffolds keep English language learners on task, helping them understand what to do.
- Scaffolds allow for a more efficient use of time. English language learners can immediately begin to work without asking for additional clarification or assistance.
- They create momentum or increase the flow of a lesson because there are fewer interruptions for clarifications and directions. (Adapted from McKenzie 2000)

In other words, scaffolds help English language learners learn new vocabulary, understand new concepts, and use new skills as they progress through the curriculum with full participation. With the help of scaffolds, students can rise to the highest levels of their capabilities.

"How do caterpillars turn into butterflies?" is the question driving a unit of study in a class full of second-grade English language learners. These students cannot wait until they have fully mastered English before they explore and receive instruction in this rigorous, high-quality unit. But since they are not proficient in English, how will they learn and then show what they know?

Their teacher, Denise, brings a live butterfly to class to spark interest and help generate research: What do they already know about butterflies? What would they like to know? After their discussion, Denise suggests important questions the students may have missed. The students then categorize their questions into those related to habitat, physical characteristics, and similar categories. Each day during the unit, these English language learners observe what is happening in the caterpillar/butterfly terrarium, read a variety of related books and articles, and share their findings orally, visually, and in writing.

Denise has structured the learning to meet the needs of all her students. First, her instruction begins where the students are cognitively and linguistically. The tasks and opportunities focus on what the students need to know and appropriate ways in which they can explain their understanding. Second, Denise uses a number of strategies. She provides a variety of reading materials (fiction and nonfiction) of varying difficulty and shows videos and video clips. Students are paired or grouped for some research activities, share with her one-on-one, and make presentations (sometimes as part of a panel) in front of the class. By scaffolding her instruction, she will give all the students opportunities to understand their learning and show what they know.

How Is This Book Organized?

This book is organized around the scaffolding concepts suggested by Walqui van Lier (2003), with some adaptations. Carol Ann Tomlinson's writing on differentiated instruction—providing a variety of ways to explore curriculum—

has also influenced our thinking about instruction for English language learners. Our work with English language learners aligns with the research that says adapting instruction according to student need helps provide a different pathway to success for struggling learners (Tomlinson 2003).

Chapter 1 provides a theoretical framework of how students learn, detailing a constructivist view of learning and discussing the theorists who have influenced the scaffolds, strategies, and lessons provided in the rest of the book.

Chapters 2 through 5 discuss specific scaffolds: modeling (Chapter 2), contextualizing (Chapter 3), developing a mental framework (Chapter 4), and reframing information (Chapter 5). We relate each scaffold to the pertinent learning or second language acquisition theories described in Chapter 1. Next, we present specific strategies that highlight the scaffold. Finally, to demonstrate how teachers can blend the strategies into their own lessons, we include complete lesson plans (for various grade levels, K–8) that we or our colleagues have taught in the classroom.

These lesson plans are similar to many used in schools today, with the addition of three important elements.

1. An English language development standard, as determined by Teachers of English to Speakers of Other Languages (TESOL). Literacy and language learning go hand in hand. This addition ensures that every lesson becomes an opportunity for English language learners to acquire more English listening, speaking, reading, and writing skills. It also helps teachers focus their instruction on clear and precise language goals to go along with their content goals.

2. An input strategy. Teachers need to consider in advance how the information or content will be presented to students. Lecture should not be the only teaching strategy used. Materials also need to be considered. With English language learners, it is essential to make the input comprehensible through visuals (including videos) and realia (objects or activities used to relate classroom teaching to real life).

3. Active learning. Here teachers consider how they will ask students to interact with the new information—discuss, debate, or question their understanding of what they are learning.

The structure of the lesson plans is summarized in Appendix C.

The final chapter, Chapter 6, discusses the specific linguistic understanding teachers need in order to teach language to English language learners. It presents strategies teachers can use to help their students develop conversational and academic language ability. In it, we:

- examine the recent attention being given to English language learners and their sustained academic success
- discuss the background of English language development and the importance of developing both conversational and academic language
- discuss vocabulary specific to academic language as well as general vocabulary used in relation to all subjects in the curriculum
- suggest literacy and standards-based lessons that include a linguistic component showing teachers how to integrate appropriate language development into their daily lessons

Chapter 6 departs from previous chapters by seeming to advocate the use of direct instruction in teaching language. There is an important reason for this: there is enormous pressure for teachers to prepare students for testing and to address the issue of underperforming English language learners. Administrators in some areas are asking teachers to submit lesson plans that show they are, in fact, teaching language. The information in this chapter will help teachers do just that.

Theoretical Bases

Constructivist Learning and Second Language Acquisition

For whatever you wish to teach, link your instructional objective to words, numbers, logic, pictures, music, the body, social interaction, and/or personal experiences of the students.

—THOMAS ARMSTRONG, *MULTIPLE INTELLIGENCES IN THE CLASSROOM*

Constructivist Learning

The scaffolds and strategies in this book are based on a constructivist view of learning. Constructivists invite students to construct their own knowledge by making meaning of their world. Learning experts such as Dewey, Piaget, Vygotsky, Gardner, and Feuerstein have been strongly influenced by constructivism (Fogarty 1999). Some of their ideas include embedding learning in real-life experiences (both inside and outside the classroom); engaging in hands-on learning (manipulating objects as a way to come to understand a concept); talking to learn (learning through social interaction); accessing different dimensions of learning (including physical action); guiding learning through teacher mediation and asking students to think about their own thinking and learning (metacognition).

Embedded Learning

John Dewey believed that the world at large is a learning experience, that the academic world inside the classroom should be connected to the world outside the classroom. He suggested that field studies and immersion in experiences stimulate learning (Dewey 1938). For example:

- Going on field trips to museums and aquariums lets students see their classroom learning come to life.
- Creating and maintaining a school garden helps students connect with a unit on local agriculture.
- Creating a model desert habitat using a child's wading pool, sand and dirt, cactuses and other succulents, and plastic desert animals makes the concept of a desert come alive for students who have never seen one.

Manipulatives: Objects to See, Touch, and Move

Swiss biologist Jean Piaget (1970) contended that children are active and motivated learners who are continually trying to make sense of the world around them. Piaget thought that children needed to be able to manipulate objects representing ideas in order to develop concepts. We often see Piaget's idea at work during math and science classes. In primary classrooms teachers provide blocks, geometric shapes, perhaps small plastic teddy bears, which students can see, touch, and move while trying to understand a particular math concept. In secondary classrooms, students might re-create the human body's internal organs using colored modeling clay in order to determine their location and functions.

Collaboration: Cooperative Learning

Elizabeth Cohen (2003) states, "To meet the challenge of heterogeneous classrooms, it is necessary for students to use each other as resources; tasks for small groups should require multiple abilities; and teachers need to know how to ensure that each student makes an important intellectual contribution to the group." Many of the strategies in this book rely heavily on social interaction because speech is a natural human attribute. According to Lev Vygotsky (1978), a Russian psychologist, learning is a very social process; as we talk, we manipulate and mediate our language and thoughts. In other words, we use language as a tool for developing thought.

Students should use language as a means toward understanding ideas and concepts. Talking is central to teaching and learning, yet many students do very little talking in school about the curriculum they are studying. Students are called on one by one to answer questions, or asked to sit quietly and listen, then work alone and silently on paper-and-pencil exercises. Talking with others in pairs, in groups, or as a whole class enables English language learners to practice speaking English and allows all students to come to a greater understanding of the ideas and concepts they are learning.

Piaget, too, believed in social interaction. He wrote that children learn about other people's thoughts and opinions by talking while they are manipulating objects (Piaget 1970). While observing groups of children working with math manipulatives, Piaget commented, "Without interchange of thought and cooperation with others the individual would never come to group [math] operations into a coherent whole" (quoted in Copeland 1974, 46).

Children's thinking improves when they are allowed to talk: people get smarter by collaborating. Therefore, teachers must provide many opportunities for students to talk and interact (in pairs, in small groups, and with the teacher) while engaging in hands-on activities. Student questions and interaction need to be encouraged.

Group work is a well-documented and highly recommended strategy for improving students' academic, cognitive, and social skills. Researchers have shown that students who consistently work in groups make better gains in academic learning and higher-order thinking than students who are taught via traditional whole-class lectures.

There is an additional benefit of cooperative work not often highlighted but essential in classrooms with students of diverse cultural backgrounds: the students' experiences in group work enable them to handle racial and social conflict issues better. Students form more lasting relationships with peers with whom they work collaboratively regardless of different ethnic backgrounds.

Cooperative learning works effectively to break down social barriers and motivate students, but it's not enough for students just to sit in groups and talk. Teachers need to adopt a model that offers structure, complexity, and potential and that uses academic language to discuss teacher-determined curriculum objectives.

For many years Spencer Kagan (1990, 1994) has provided inservice training sessions for teachers on how to implement the cooperative structures he has created (team building, class building, communication building, information exchange, and mastery/thinking skills) through activities such as inside/outside circle, think-pair-share, and three-step interview. His structures, which focus on organizing interaction, not on the content taught within the structure, form a basis for cooperative group work.

Elizabeth Cohen and R. Lotan (1997) have created a novel program called "complex instruction" in which English language learners acquire conversational English, develop academic language, and expand their content area knowledge through cooperative learning. The program asks teachers to create discovery-based, curriculum-aligned projects that students complete in groups. Cohen delegates authority to students, thus making them responsible for their own learning. They develop a positive interdependence on one another and serve as language role models and resources for one another. She also addresses status problems in the classroom in that the learning projects are designed so that no one individual can complete the project alone. Each member of the group is valued for what he or she contributes. In many classrooms, English language learners are perceived as less competent and given fewer opportunities to participate, and so learn less. In Cohen's complex instruction English language learners bring strength to the group, and their participation is needed for the project to succeed.

Multidimensional Learning: Drawing on Students' Strengths

Learning research has stressed that the brain processes information through visual, auditory, and kinesthetic pathways (Grinder 1995). Visual learners *see* the world. They create and store images by reading, writing, drawing, and designing. Auditory learners *hear* the world. They create and store voices and sounds by listening, speaking, singing, and chanting. Kinesthetic learners *sense* the world. They create and store feelings, sensations, and body motions by moving, touching, making things, experiencing, and acting. Being aware of these three modes of learning helps teachers plan instruction to best help students learn and strengthens the case for teaching strategies that include more than whole-class lectures and individual worksheets.

Howard Gardner (1983), a professor at Harvard University, has designed a "multiple intelligences" instruction model based on the broad range of human abilities. His eight intelligences—linguistic, logical/mathematic, spatial, musical, bodily/kinesthetic, interpersonal, intrapersonal, and naturalist—represent the many ways that people learn. As people solve problems in the real world, they tap into their different intelligences and combine them in multiple ways to express their own understanding.

Thomas Armstrong, in his book *Multiple Intelligences in the Classroom* (1994), refines Gardner's ideas and puts them into practice in the classroom in novel and exciting ways. One of his examples is teaching first graders how to tell time by matching a number of intelligences with students' learning styles. He begins by telling a fictional story of a land without clocks in which children stand on a mountaintop and chant a rhyme about time that includes each hour of the day. After telling the story, Armstrong asks students to map out a huge circle on the carpet to represent a handless clock and then has them indicate the different hour designations using their bodies and hands. Next, they create a "clock dance" to the music of Bill Haley's "Rock Around the Clock." At their desks they write their own stories about the land with no clocks and illustrate them with clock faces depicting varying times. They conclude the activity by sharing their stories and illustrations with their classmates.

Physical Action: Moving to Learn

Every teacher has students who squirm, who need to touch things, who want to build things. These are the students who are always getting up and moving around the room or reaching inside their desks for something with which to play. Learning for these students is connected to Gardner's idea (1983) of bodily/kinesthetic intelligence.

Armstrong's research (1994) substantiates that there is a neurological connection between physical movement and language and literacy. While this belief is not well accepted by linguists, teachers instinctively know that some students learn while in motion. Acting out words, role-playing, using pantomime, working with clay, singing, dancing, chanting, working within a group—all are classroom strategies that get students moving while learning. In addition, some students need to be able to manipulate things while processing their learning (Piaget 1970). These activities can help students learn and remember their learning, and teachers need to include them in their teaching repertoires. (That they are also fun and engage students is a wonderful bonus!)

Mediated Learning and Metacognition: The Teacher as Guide

Reuven Feuerstein (1980) believed that students learn through discovery accompanied by skillful teacher intervention or mediation. In the following classroom example, a teacher mediates a student's understanding of a math problem after the student has abandoned his attempts to solve it and asks for help. Instead of telling the student the answer or advising him to go back and look at the problem again, the teacher uses a questioning strategy:

STUDENT: I need help on this problem. I get to a certain point and then I'm stuck.

TEACHER: Tell me your thinking up to this point. Why did you put down the answer you have?

STUDENT: I don't know why.

TEACHER: Think back to the problems we worked together yesterday. How does this remind you of what we did? Do you have a good reason for doing what you did here on your problem today? Tell me what you were thinking.

Metacognition is the term used to describe becoming conscious of your own thinking and reflecting on it. When students are aware of their own thinking patterns, they can develop effective learning strategies (Feuerstein 1980). Teachers can help students develop metacognition by voicing their own thinking as they teach. For example, when teaching revision in the writing process, you would explain, by voicing what you are thinking, exactly the changes you are going to make to a piece you have written and why.

Second Language Acquisition

A ninth-grade immigrant girl once said:

> I just sat in my classes and didn't understand anything. Sometimes I would try to think about a happy time when I didn't feel stupid. My teachers never called on me or talked to me. I think they either forgot I was there or else wished I wasn't. I waited and waited, thinking that someday I will know English. (Olsen 1988, 62)

This indictment of our educational system is just as valid today as it was in the past. When students enter school knowing only a language other than English and are put into classrooms where the language of instruction is English, they simply do not understand what is being taught.

Human beings have created language as a means of representing the world and their experiences within it. If students in English language classrooms cannot speak, read, or write in English, they cannot participate in class or group discussions. They cannot understand what they read or express their thoughts in writing. The scaffolds in the following chapters help students develop the academic language they need to be successful in school.

Background Knowledge

Jim Cummins (1989) helps us understand the important bridge provided by background knowledge. He believes that prior knowledge and experience are the foundation for understanding new information. In any classroom, but especially those that include English language learners, students' prior knowledge about a topic will vary widely. Finding out what students know about a particular topic before instruction begins allows teachers to supply vocabulary and factual information that will be important for understanding the new learning. For example, a junior high social science teacher beginning a unit on Japan might prepare students for the lesson by bringing in Japanese artifacts and photographs and allowing small groups of students to discuss what they already know about Japan. Building on this understanding, students will be able to understand ever more complex language and tackle ever more demanding academic activities.

Conversational Versus Academic Language Proficiency

Another important concept for educators to understand is that of conversational versus academic language proficiency. *Conversational language* is the everyday language used for basic communication. *Academic language* is language used as an "instrument for thought in problem solving" (Skutnabb-Kangas 1981, 111). Many times students are believed to "know" a language when they demonstrate conversational fluency, and instructional decisions are made based on this inaccuracy. In any case, as students progress through school, they are asked to use language in increasingly more cognitively demanding ways.

Robin Scarcella's research (2003) shows that little attention has been given to academic language in elementary and secondary schools and that the literature on teaching language through the content areas has focused more on techniques than on the development of academic language. According to Scarcella, in the last ten years teachers have moved away from teaching the features of the English language explicitly as well as from assessing the development of those skills. Students need a firm foundation in English so they can achieve the goals of a challenging academic curriculum.

Scarcella defines literacy as the ability to develop advanced levels of proficiency in the four modes of language: reading, writing, listening, and speaking. Academic English allows students to read and understand complex words and use those words in spoken and written communication (10). Scarcella's framework for academic language development focuses on different aspects of the linguistic, cognitive, and sociocultural/psychological dimensions of academic English. She states: "The lexical component of English and its associated features used in academic situations is the knowledge of the forms and meanings of words that are used across academic disciplines" (12). The cognitive dimension of academic language includes knowledge, higher-order thinking skills, and cognitive and metalinguistic strategies. The component of higher-order thinking develops students' abilities to work with academic texts for specific disciplines.

The Acquisition-Versus-Learning Hypothesis

Stephen Krashen (1985) suggests that people have two different ways to gain ability in a language. *Acquisition* is a subconscious process very similar to the way in which a first language is learned. The learner is not aware of it while it is happening (and may not be aware of the results); he or she is only aware of using the language for some purpose, such as having a conversation, watching a movie, or going shopping. Krashen also suggests that language can be acquired while reading. Since people are able to read much faster than they can speak, written language is a better source for language acquisition than oral language is.

Learning a language, on the other hand, produces conscious knowledge. Language is learned by memorizing words and completing grammar exercises. Students are taught specific structures of the language, such as the subjunctive tense, in carefully sequenced drills. This is how a second language is taught in most classrooms. But researchers like Krashen have discovered that most language is acquired, not learned, so teachers can better set aside grammar drills and focus on strategies that foster acquisition.

The Input Hypothesis and Cognitive Development

Krashen (1985) also hypothesizes that people acquire language in only one way, by understanding messages—that is, through *comprehensible input*. Comprehensible input appears to be missing in most current methods of instructing English language learners. Students are taught curriculum without the use of strategies that help them understand the message the teacher is sending. Lectures and drills do not provide enough understandable messages. Krashen sums up his hypotheses by saying that English language learners acquire language when they receive interesting, understandable messages in an anxiety-free environment.

Providing comprehensible input is not difficult but can take more preparation than some teachers are willing to undertake. Looking for color photographs to illustrate a story, bringing in real-world objects or activities that will help explain a social studies concept, and using a video clip to make background information related to a literature selection come alive are all ways to add clues to meaning, to *contextualize* instruction.

As touched on earlier, Krashen also believes that cognitive development is incidental and happens without the learner's conscious knowledge. Cognitive development occurs when people attempt to solve problems of interest to them and are engaged in critical thinking in specific situations. For that to happen teachers should use strategies that enhance their students' understanding of the concepts taught.

Other researchers also see writing, discussion, and cooperative learning as enhancers of cognitive development. Students can write to themselves to clarify difficult problems and stimulate their thinking (Applebee 1978). Meaning is not what you started out with when you began to write but all the new ideas and elaborated thoughts that remain at the end.

Let's watch how Sandra encourages cognitive development during a letter-writing lesson. She has already taught persuasive writing and sees an opportunity to ask her students to use it to solve a problem: the principal has taken away the students' Snack Shack privileges and they are upset about it. Sandra introduces letter writing, another third/fourth-grade requirement, combining it with what the students already know about persuasive writing and with problem solving. She asks the students, in small groups, to discuss ways to persuade the principal to change her mind and allow students to buy treats at recess. They include the best arguments in letters that they then hand deliver to the principal. The assignment has a happy ending: because of the novel way in which they have approached the problem, the principal reinstates their privileges!

The Importance of Output

Just as Krashen (1985) says that second language learners need comprehensible input for learning to take place, Swain (1985) claims that second language learners also need the opportunity to produce output. She explains that students who have been learning a second language in classes where the teachers do all the talking do not reach a high degree of proficiency in the target language. Her conclusion is that second language learners need to interact frequently with native speakers of the language. Therefore, collaborative work is a key element in second language instruction (Freeman and Freeman 2001).

We see Swain's hypothesis in action in Sandra's immigration unit as students organize and present a recipe for a dish native to a country they are studying. The students interact with native speakers in obtaining the recipe in an authentic situation but unconsciously use English when they demonstrate how to prepare the dish.

Contextualized and Decontextualized Learning

Cummins (1981, 1996) and Snow et al. (1991) have pointed out that the difference between contextualized and decontextualized language is important in understanding the nature of children's language proficiency and literacy development. Contextualized language is communicated and supported by contextual or interpersonal cues such as gestures, facial expressions, and intonation. Decontextualized language uses linguistic cues independent of the immediate communicative context. Students who are unfamiliar with those linguistic cues have difficulty interpreting meaning in decontextualized settings.

Pauline Gibbons (1991) has made a distinction between what she calls *playground language* and *classroom language*. The first term refers to the language used by students to make friends and to participate in daily activities that develop and maintain social relationships. This kind of language is developed during face-to-face contact and uses gestures, visuals, and other aids that enhance understanding in a particular situation. Playground language is an important part of second language development because it helps children interact with their peers in everyday social life, but it is very different from the type of language students encounter in classrooms. The academic demands of classroom language require developed critical thinking skills in the target language. Without the ability to use and understand classroom language, second language learners' potential in academic areas is very limited.

The distinction between contextualized and decontextualized language, or between playground language and classroom language, leads Cummins (1981) to make a distinction between what he calls *basic interpersonal communicative skills* (BICS) and *cognitive academic language proficiency* (CALP). Teachers need to understand that academic challenges are important for students' growth, but contextual support must also be present in the activities if students are to succeed academically (Cummins 1996).

Here's an example from Denise's classroom that addresses comprehensible input, contextualized learning, and the affective filter. For a social studies lesson on agriculture in the valley where the students live, she reads aloud *Working Cotton*, by Sherley Anne Williams (1992), which features a character who as a child picked cotton with her family. After reading the book Denise passes around a sample of handpicked cotton. To further contextualize her students' understanding, she displays a sweater, skirt, and other clothing made of cotton, labeling them so students will learn the basic vocabulary as well as the academic language related to the unit of study.

Teaching Language Through Content and Developing All Modes of Language

Based on a study of his own son's language development, Michael Halliday (1973) has suggested that people *learn* language (how to speak, read, and write it), learn *through* language (all about the world inside and outside the classroom), and learn *about* language (phonics, grammar, spelling) as they develop their skills as literate beings. They do this all at the same time. The Freemans refer to this as learning language as it is being used (Freeman and Freeman 1998). Students assimilate grammar, syntax, and semantic information when they are learning about history, science, or math, as language is repeated naturally across disciplines.

Here's an example of learning language through content. Using her district's fifth-grade content standards, Sandra develops a unit on immigration that has three interrelated topics: immigrants of yesterday and today, multiculturalism, and geography. As her students learn the facts and specific vocabulary related to the influx of immigrants to the United States throughout history, they also learn geographic terminology related to where the immigrants came from and where they settled. The students then move on to the idea of multiculturalism and its vocabulary, first within the community in which the students live, then, using Cinderella stories from around the world, in the places where the stories are set. Throughout the unit the academic vocabulary specific to immigration is used continually, and concepts are developed through writing, listening, and speaking.

Understanding academic language and using it effectively in academic settings is essential for English language learners and native speakers of English alike. Few students come to school with the language necessary to perform fully as educated people, to engage in academic discussions and read and understand the textbooks used in their classes. Using supportive strategies, teachers must help students develop the academic language they need to be successful in school.

Modeling

Show Them, Help Them, Let Them Do It

I understand the importance of communicating the steps of a process in a clear and demonstrable way for English language learners. I know that even native English speakers need modeling of new tasks, and for English language learners virtually everything is new. Sometimes I rush through things to make up time. Some students understand the task, others figure it out along the way, and my English language learners may not get it at all. It is good to remember that modeling is so important.

—AMY, BEGINNING TEACHER

Modeling is an important part of instruction, and most teachers are familiar with the process and try to use it. However, pressed to teach more in less time or worn down during a long day of teaching, they may neglect modeling in favor of creating time for more academic activities. This is usually a mistake, especially with English language learners.

Vygotsky (1978) suggests that in order to participate fully and meaningfully in our culture, we learn ways of doing and thinking from more capable others in collaborative activities. The expert or teacher understands what the novice or student knows, and helps guide the novice to a higher level of understanding. One reason modeling is an effective scaffold is that students make meaningful cognitive connections through direct experience (Bandura 1986). It helps students avoid the confusion that results from misunderstanding oral instructions. Modeling gives students a more concrete understanding and lays a foundation for later mastery of the task or process.

In modeling, the teacher (or a knowledgeable peer) shows students the desired behavior, skill, or process as the students follow along and then try it for themselves. Only the most important steps and decisions are stressed. Modeling can be accomplished in different ways. Teachers can work through the steps in a process or present an example of a completed project. They can model before teaching the lesson, during the lesson, or at the end.

Thinking Aloud

English language learners can be shut out from acquiring the thinking and problem-solving processes involved in reading and writing. The key to understanding for English language learners is modeling accompanied by thinking aloud. Thinking aloud helps clue English language learners in so that they can understand and complete an assignment, as the other students do.

Modeling the thought processes in accomplishing a task, executing a skill, or exhibiting a behavior can take some getting used to. We are not normally aware of the thinking and monitoring we do. It takes practice to become comfortable with the process, but it is well worth the effort.

Think-alouds are carefully structured to show how users of an effective strategy think and monitor their understanding (Baumann, Jones, and Seifert-Kessell 1993). This information is not readily available; studies have shown that English language learners and struggling readers will not use effective strategies unless teachers model their thinking processes for them (Israel 2002; Pressley and Afflerbach 1995). The think-aloud consists of teachers voicing their thinking and problem solving out loud for the students to hear. By showing students how an expert does it, teachers open up pathways for the students' own thinking.

English language learners really do want to improve their reading abilities and become more successful at school. Sometimes they misbehave and develop bad attitudes to cover up a lack of skills. Garcia (2002) and Block (2003) suggest that teachers can build students' reading comprehension, decoding skills, vocabulary, and fluency through think-alouds that address those areas of reading. Block (2004) and Oster (2001) suggest that think-alouds significantly increase comprehension test scores, encourage students' belief in their own understanding, and help students choose thinking processes that enable them to overcome reading comprehension challenges.

LESSON PLAN: STORY ELEMENTS

Grade Level: Third grade

English Language Learner Suitability: Intermediate and advanced

Objective: Each student will identify an appropriate idea for a story, one that contains the essential elements of character, setting, problem, and resolution.

IRA/NCTE English Language Arts Standard 4: Students adjust their use of spoken, written, and visual language . . . to communicate effectively with a variety of audiences for different purposes.

National TESOL Goal 2, Standard 2: To use English to achieve academically in all content areas. Students will use English to obtain, process, construct, and provide subject matter information in spoken and written form.

Materials

Poster displaying these questions to ask about a story:

1. Who are the characters?
2. Where did the story take place?
3. What was the problem?
4. How was the problem solved?
5. What can we learn from what happened?
6. Are any parts not clear?

Overview

Some students have difficulty producing stories that contain all the essential elements because they may not be consciously aware of these elements, what they consist of, and what they mean. For example, they may fail to develop the problem and solution adequately and end up with an incident rather than a story. Students develop their stories more fully and make better use of language when they are first asked to talk about and revise a story idea. One way this lesson supports English language learners is by giving them the opportunity to try different vocabulary and sentence structures and hear them modeled correctly in an authentic situation.

In this lesson, you model taking an incident that really happened and turning it into a story. Choose something to which students can relate (for example, a European vacation cruise would not be suitable). Ask the students to listen for essential story elements such as characters, setting, problem, and resolution of the problem. When you finish relating the incident, have the students quiz you about whether all the essential story elements are present. If they are, you can use subsequent lessons to model sketching out the story and writing, editing, and revising it. If they are not, add the elements that are missing.

Procedure

1. Ask the students to gather around you, sitting either on the floor or in chairs.
2. Since making connections to emotions evokes ideas for stories, choose an incident in which you were scared, embarrassed, elated, or hurt. Use a chart of faces showing the different emotions and point to the appropriate one.
3. Begin thinking aloud about the incident. You might purposely leave out or under-develop a story element or two. In the following example, Denise doesn't describe the characters and the setting in enough detail.

> I need to think about a time I was afraid. When I saw my brothers over the weekend they told me something I didn't know about a trip to Mexico when we were young. My nephew was curious to know if his dad had ever done anything naughty when he was young, and my older brother confessed that he had. Since what my brother did was related to a situation in which I was afraid, I'll tell you about it.
>
> A long time ago when I was five and getting ready to start the first grade, my mother, father, older brother, younger brother, and I visited a ranch in Durango, Mexico. This was the town where my father grew up, and he had many fond memories of the time he spent there. The ranch was out of town and had many animals on it. One of the men who

worked at the ranch thought it would be fun for my brothers and me to ride a burro. I was put on the burro first and was riding the burro, letting it roam wherever it wanted to—I almost started to say the burro took off running, but I need to keep the events in the order that they happened so I'll talk about what my brothers were doing—I was unable to see where my father was and what my brothers were doing because I was so concerned with the burro and what it was doing. I was afraid to be on it. [*Denise refers to the drawing of a scared face here.*] I knew my brothers were standing close to the burro and me. All of a sudden the burro began to run and headed down switchbacks into a deep canyon lined with prickly bushes. I frantically began to try to stop the burro, but it was no use. I was too little to know what I was doing or be able to handle an animal that bolted for the canyon. My father yelled at some of the ranch hands in Spanish, and they started to run after us. They caught up with us and walked the burro back to where we were previously. I was safe again and all was well.

Last weekend, which was many years after this happened, my older brother told me that he had hit the burro in the rump hard, just to see what would happen. He never realized it would make the burro run away or create an unsafe situation for me. The fact that he had encouraged the burro to run off was the piece of information that had been missing all these years. Now it made sense to me why the burro ran away. I never realized that my brother was capable of causing me harm by playing a trick on me, but now I know that just playing around can create a dangerous situation.

Now, you need to ask me the questions on the poster so we can check to see if what happened to me is something I can turn into a written story.

4. Let students ask you the questions displayed on the chart. In Denise's lesson, her students want additional information about the characters (*Where is your mother? What did your brothers look like? Why don't they have names?*) and about where the story takes place (*What part of Mexico is Durango? What did the ranch look like? Were there any other animals around?*). Denise needs to retell those parts, adding descriptive information. Here's what she says:

Okay, we agree that the story parts are in place. We know from our reading that a character's traits and feelings, the qualities that define a particular character, are central to stories. They tend to drive the story's problem or shape the outcome of the story, so while I am telling this story, I need to go back and say more about the characters, my mom, dad, older brother, younger brother, and me. I also need to describe the ranch more. I can think about what I saw, heard, smelled, and felt, so I can add more description of the ranch. By telling more about the characters and describing the setting more I'll be making the background stronger and my story will be better.

5. Next, the teacher provides an opportunity for students to get a feel for how they will do this themselves with a partner. The process should be modeled by two students while the rest of the students observe and note what went well and what was left out. This is called the fish bowl strategy (Baloche et al. 1993). Call attention if the teller strays off track and begins talking about something else or if the listener is not listening. Comment on good listening behavior: looking at the other person, sitting up straight, leaning in with interest. When the teller is finished, have his or her partner ask the questions listed on the story elements poster and request needed clarification. Ask the students who are observing what went well and what could be improved. Be sensitive to students who may feel afraid about sharing or about not knowing enough English to tell a long, involved story.

6. Have all the students, in pairs, tell a story idea to a partner.

Assessment

Monitor ongoing progress. Since the students do not yet have a written product, move about the room, listening to and watching the behavior of the student pairs to get a sense of whether students have understood what they've been asked to do. Work with pairs of students if they are not achieving the objectives of the lesson.

Advantages for English Language Learners

To modify this lesson to include beginning English language learners, Denise could contextualize it (see Chapter 3) by showing pictures of a desert ranch when she describes the setting, thus providing visual clues to the setting and the emotions central to the story. She could make animal sounds and use gestures or body language to describe riding the burro before and after it started running. She could also use labeled figures, either toys or cutouts, to model the story action. Beginning English speakers can draw sequential pictures of their story and label them. Another advantage is that students can verbalize what they will write before actually doing it. They have the opportunity to try different vocabulary and sentence structures and hear them modeled correctly by a partner in an authentic situation.

Reading Informational Text (Nonfiction)

We are an information society. A large percentage of what we read as adults is nonfiction: newspapers, magazines, bus schedules, TV listings, directions for assembling products, text on a computer screen, recipes, and so on. A large percentage of questions on standardized tests relative to comprehension are based on passages of nonfiction text. Successful negotiation of nonfiction text is critical to success in education and in life. Students who use the same strategies to read nonfiction as they use to read fiction experience problems. Understanding the differences between fiction and nonfiction and adopting new strategies specific to nonfiction helps students be more successful in comprehending all kinds of text.

Nonfiction explains facts and concepts. Its purpose is to inform, describe, or report. English language learners are challenged by nonfiction for a variety of reasons. Content material is usually covered very quickly. The vocabulary presents huge problems, and there may be specialized expressions for a particular area of study. Perhaps there are too many concepts explained on each page of a science text. The visuals that help students interpret the text may be confusing and difficult to understand. The sentences in science textbooks are usually complex and are often cast in the passive tense. Also, a student's culture may not have prepared him or her to draw conclusions.

Students need to vary their reading of nonfiction to accommodate their purpose. Sometimes they will read the text from start to finish; sometimes they will read only the part containing the specific information they are seeking. Students need to know how nonfiction is organized, how to locate information in the text, and how to interpret that information. Nonfiction text features and their functions need to be taught to students within the context in which they will be used. Too often they are taught in isolation, and students do not understand why they need to know this information and how it can help them become better readers and writers.

Titles and headings; boldface, italic, and colored print; numbered and bulleted lists; and captions and labels help students locate information. Diagrams, cutaways, cross sections, overlays, maps, word bubbles, charts, tables, graphs, framed text, sidebars, illustrations, and photographs help students interpret information. Text organizers such as the index, preface, table of contents, glossary, and the appendix help students find the specific information they're looking for.

Students also need to understand how ideas are organized in nonfiction. Being aware of these structures helps students understand what they are reading and organize their thoughts in writing (Robb 2003). The five most common expository text structures are description, sequence, comparison and contrast, cause and effect, and problem and solution (Meyer and Freedle 1984). Specific graphic organizers can be used with each of these structures to help students visually organize the ideas being presented (Smith and Tompkins 1988). Filling in a graphic organizer after reading a text or creating one before writing a text helps students understand what they have read and makes their writing more coherent. Graphic organizers are also a way for teachers to check student comprehension. Beginning English language learners can express what they know with a graphic organizer even when they may be completely unable to write sentences or paragraphs to convey that understanding.

For description, an effective graphic organizer is a web or a cluster—something that organizes words and ideas in categories and subcategories around a topic in a way that defines information (see Chapter 4). Timelines and summaries work well with chronological sequence. Similarities and differences among facts, people, and/or events (comparison and contrast) can be plotted on a classic Venn diagram or a two-column chart. The cause-and-effect structure, which describes how one thing occurs as the result of another, can be shown using flowcharts, chain sequences, and cycle graphs. Text identifying a problem and posing one or more solutions can be charted on semantic maps or any kind of diagram that depicts decision making.

It's also very helpful if students are familiar with some of the cue or indicator words that signal a particular text structure. Words that signal description are *to begin with, in fact, for instance*; sequence, *on [date], not long after, now, first, second*; comparison and contrast, *however, but, either/or, while*; cause and effect or problem and solution, *therefore, since, consequently, as a result*.

A Think-Aloud About Text Structure

To show teachers how to apply some of what we have been discussing, we offer an example from the information children's book, *How Is a Crayon Made?* (Charles 1988). This book shows the text structure of sequencing. In a think-aloud, the teacher models finding the important ideas of the book, one page or section at a time. The teacher looks for information in sequence, such as dates that show important events. The cue words are those such as *on (date)*, *not long after, now, as before, first*, and *second*.

1. *Teacher*: When you read there is a voice inside your head that is your reading, but there is also a voice inside your brain that is saying what you think about what you read. I'm going to tell you that thinking while I read.

2. I know that authors organize nonfiction books in special ways. One of those ways is sequence, where the author puts information in a certain order. I already know some sequences such as the months of the year and the days of the week. I will be looking for the sequence structure.

3. I first will look at the title and the picture. They work together to tell me the book has something to do with crayons. There is no subheading, so the title doesn't tell me in any more detail what the book is about. The first sentence is a detail that is not important. It asks me to think about a world without crayons. (*The teacher continues reading.*)

4. The first sentence of the next paragraph tells an important idea, that the first step in making a crayon is creating a color. There is a cue word, *first*. This tells me that the text structure may be sequential. I need to pay attention to it because it tells me that making a crayon is a *process* that will have steps to it.

5. As I continue reading, the next thing I see is a photograph of a man in front of a big machine scraping something off a screen. I know I need to look more closely at the details because a photograph will give me extra information that the words in the book will not. I see everything is the color purple. I am thinking that this work is messy and looks hard to do.

6. Next, I come across the word *next*, another cue word that tells me the structure is sequential. Now I know the information will be presented. I would organize this information in a graphic organizer that has boxes with an arrow leading from one box to the next in a chain.

The teacher continues modeling, being careful to not take too much time. Fifteen minutes total is about all that students can handle per modeling/think-aloud lesson. Depending on the difficulty and the age of the informational book I choose to read, there will be more text features to highlight. I will want to make sure to start out simple and model one or two at a time. The same goes for text structures. I can begin as early as second grade with the example above and move all the way to eighth grade, increasing the text structures and features appropriate for the ages of the students.

Teacher modeling in a think-aloud manner alerts students to what the focus is, what the text tells them, and how the book is organized for comprehension. This is an important step before asking students to find the structure on their own or make a graphic organizer containing the information from the book. Generally teachers spend lots of time *telling* students how to do things and very little to no time *showing* students what to look for and how to do something. That is why the think-aloud is so powerful. It bridges the gap between telling students what to do and having students do it themselves. After students master the think-aloud, they are ready to find the different structures themselves in written text.

LESSON PLAN:
CAUSE-AND-EFFECT TEXT STRUCTURE

Grade Level: Seventh grade

English Language Learner Suitability: Intermediate through advanced

Objective: Students will analyze cause-and-effect nonfiction and thus improve their reading comprehension. Students will use a graphic organizer to put abstract ideas from the text into a concrete form.

IRA/NCTE English Language Arts Standard 3: Students apply a wide range of literature from many periods in many genres to build an understanding of the many dimensions . . . of human experience.

National TESOL Goal 2, Standard 2: To use English to achieve academically in all content areas. Students will use English to obtain, process, construct, and provide subject matter information in spoken and written form.

Materials

- Selected pages of a science article (on overhead transparencies) that uses the cause-and-effect structure. Alternatively, you can use an easy-to-read science book. In either case, the text should be accessible enough so that students can focus on understanding the structure without being distracted by trying to understand what the text says.
- A graphic organizer that complements the cause-and-effect structure.

Procedure

1. Lead students through the material, focusing on identifying the cause-and-effect text structure rather than understanding the content. In the following example, Ed chooses a short, easy-to-read informational booklet on oceans published by National Geographic.

> I know that when I read I think about things that happen and why those things happen. First, I'm going to model for you one of the text structures of nonfiction, cause and effect. I know that things that happen are called *effects* and that why they happen is called the *cause*. So I will be looking for things that happen and why they happen.
>
> Looking at Chapter 1, The Open Ocean, I see a heading in a large font, or print, that says "Motion and Might." The author is saying that oceans are mighty and move. This makes sense when I look at the photograph of a huge wave pounding against a lighthouse. The photograph supports what the chapter heading says.
>
> [*Ed reads two paragraphs that discuss currents.*]
>
> I see that the words *surface currents* are in bold type. This means the term is important, and a definition of a surface current follows. As I read on I see more boldface words, *deep ocean current*, and know that this is a second kind of current flowing in the ocean. Then the author gives a definition, just as he did for surface currents. If currents flow in the ocean, then I'm wondering why. "What causes these two kinds of currents?" I ask myself. I remember that just after the definition of surface currents the author tells what causes them: "The wind and the rotation of the Earth create surface currents." So if surface currents flow in the ocean it's because of the wind and the rotation of the Earth.

I'm going to reread the information right after the discussion of surface currents to find out what causes deep ocean currents. It says that
when very cold water sinks under warm water, this movement causes a
deep water current. So now I know what causes both kinds of currents
and why they flow in the ocean.

2. Create a graphic organizer to help the students understand what the words of the
    text are explaining. Ed and his students create this one:

Effect: What happens?	Cause: Why does it happen?
Two kinds of currents flow through the oceans.	The wind and the Earth's rotation create surface currents. The movement of very cold water meeting warm water causes deep water currents.

3. Ask the students to write for three minutes about what they learned about the
    cause-and-effect text structure and what they now understand about how to use
    this information to negotiate text. Suggest that labels may help them organize
    their writing.
4. In succeeding lessons, you can guide students to find other cause-and-effect rela-
    tionships, either further on in the same material or in new material. Encourage
    them to model their own thinking after your earlier think-aloud.
5. If ready, students can tackle a simple text on their own.

Assessment

The assessment is the quick write. It guides your instruction by revealing whether or
not students understand and whether you should model this process again or move on
to something else.

Advantages for English Language Learners

Make sure to point out the visuals in the book or article, and use gestures or draw on
the whiteboard as you are reading and articulating your thought processes. Less proficient English language learners can substitute a quick draw for a quick write. Beginning English language learners can draw the cause-and-effect graphic organizer.

Final Thoughts on Teaching Nonfiction Text

With so much information being conveyed in nonfiction text, how does a
reader know what to focus on and where to begin teaching students how to

read this type of text? The following are some suggestions for teaching English language learners to read expository text.

1. Read only one section at a time.
2. Look for key words in the title and in all the headings and subheadings; these help you anticipate what you will be reading about.
3. Study the text features: words in bold print signal main ideas.
4. Connect all the pictures, charts, diagrams, and so on with the main ideas.
5. Reread the first and last sentences in each paragraph: nonfiction writers put important information there. Separate the important information from details that may be interesting but are not vital to understanding the concept.
6. Identify the text structure; knowing this organizational pattern will help you find the specific information you need.
7. Remember to think as you read!

The Chapter in a Nutshell

Scaffold: Modeling

Teachers show students the desired behavior, skill, or process so that students can follow along and then try it for themselves.

Appropriate grade levels: K–2 (modified), 3–5, 6–8

Strategies
    Think-aloud
    Fish bowl

Content area
- Social studies
- Math
- Science
- Reading/language arts
- Reading
- Writing
- Listening
- Speaking
- Language processes

How is it done?

Think–aloud: Teachers model their thinking and problem solving out loud for students to hear, showing them how an expert does it. This opens pathways for student thinking.

Fish bowl: Teachers ask a student (or group of students) to model while the rest of the class forms a circle and observes. Afterward the entire group discusses strengths and weaknesses.

Why is the scaffold important to use?

The scaffold models for students what and how to verbalize what they are thinking before they are asked to write. It clues them in as to what needs to be verbalized.

Contextualizing

Provide Clues to Meaning

Junior high teacher Ed Thurston used to teach history very traditionally. He began his lessons with a lecture. Next he called on his fluent readers to read aloud one or two paragraphs from a section or chapter (or occasionally did so himself). After the reading, Ed asked the students, individually, to write out answers to the questions at the end of the chapter or turn in a written summary. What they were not able to finish in class became homework. This was his daily routine. Overall, his students were able to remember a fair amount of what they had heard and read in class; this information, in connection with the studying they did at home, allowed them to perform well on the chapter tests.

But then things changed, and this way of teaching no longer worked. First, an influx of English language learners in his classes meant his students were not all fluent English speakers, readers, and writers. These students had difficulty making sense of what Ed taught and did not do well on the chapter tests. Next, the principal began to demand higher test scores, insisting that all students make verifiable progress in their learning. There were also new state standards with which to contend. Ed felt pressured to see that his English language learners did well in class and that all his students were able to show what they were learning on the new standards-based assessments.

Although Ed didn't realize it, his lessons lacked *context*. To make history comprehensible to his students he needed to use props and visuals, include collaborative problem solving, and allow his students to "move to learn" rather than remain glued to their desks. Simple techniques like these add clues to the language of the textbook and promote greater understanding in every student.

Aida Walqui van Lier (2003) describes contextualization as instruction that clarifies new concepts by explaining them within a sensory environment that includes props, real-life activities, all kinds of visuals (including videos), manipulatives to see and touch, collaborative grouping, and physical movement. This additional sensory information is not present in traditional lectures and question/answer activities.

Visuals

Contextualizing by adding visuals to a reading lesson can have a tremendous impact on comprehension. Primary teachers generally understand the value of visuals and routinely use them in their instruction. The illustrations in the picture books they read aloud help convey the meaning of the text. They may also use pictures or props as a way to help students understand the sequence of events or anything else students have difficulty grasping. Visuals should become an integral part of all teachers' repertoire of strategies. When visuals are used in instruction, the lesson becomes more engaging.

Pictures, sketches, and illustrations are instructional tools to help students create visual images and store and retrieve information they have read. Miller (2002) suggests that making mind pictures challenges the students to look inward and become consciously aware of their mental images and thinking. This can be particularly helpful for English language learners when they are asked to listen to lectures and take notes or to read a chapter and answer questions. Visuals can help students build the background knowledge necessary to understand a new skill, idea, or concept.

Here's an example of using visuals to enhance reading comprehension. Before Sandra's fifth graders read a short story by Gary Soto (1995) about a boy attending a pool party on a hot summer day, Sandra shows them pictures she has taken at a public swimming pool. The students discuss the activities going on at the pool (jumping off the diving board, horseplay, water games) and the related vocabulary (*lifeguard*, *beach towels*, *dive*). With these clues, the students can access knowledge and experiences they already have in order to understand the reading to come. In addition, this discussion provides an opportunity for English language learners to practice using pool-related vocabulary they may not know or be sure about (*diving board*, *inner tube*, *drowning*).

Movies and Videos

Researchers have recently begun exploring the video–literacy connection. A movie version of a book can powerfully support English learners' reading comprehension by providing clues about when and where events take place and conveying a myriad of details that may go unnoticed when students are reading the text (Hibbing and Rankin-Erickson 2003). Finding the best ways to use videos can be difficult, however: teachers sometimes see videos as a culminating celebration, and parents and administrators may see them as unrelated to school curricula. Many teachers show parts of a video (with or without sound) before or as students read the related portion of the text.

—— LESSON PLAN: BREATHING LIFE INTO TEACHING ——

Grade Level: Eighth grade

English Language Learner Suitability: Intermediate and advanced

Objective: This lesson will help students activate their prior knowledge before reading *The Outsiders* (Hinton 1967). They will infer traits of the characters by watching the movie version of the book and using a graphic organizer.

IRA/NCTE English Language Arts Standard 1: Students read a wide range of print and nonprint texts to build an understanding of texts, of themselves, and of the cultures of the United States and the world; to acquire new information; to respond to the needs and demands of society and the workplace; and for personal fulfillment.

National TESOL Goal 2, Standard 2: To use English to achieve academically in all content areas. Students will use English to obtain, process, construct, and provide subject matter information in spoken and written form.

Materials

- A videotape of *The Outsiders*
- A minute timer
- A character map
- A pen

Procedure

1. Show a ten-minute clip from the movie. Ask students to take notes specifically on the characters: Who are they? What do they talk about? What kinds of things do they do?
2. Have students, in groups of four, discuss what they noticed, and add things other group members have noticed to their own notes.
3. Show another fifteen minutes of the movie, having students add to their notes.
4. Hand out copies of the blank character map, explain how to use it, and have students enter the names of the characters.

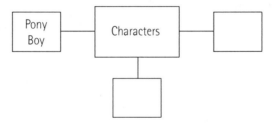

5. Show ten more minutes of the movie.
6. In groups, have students discuss the traits of the characters and extend the character map by adding these traits.

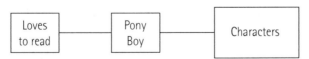

7. Tell students that the traits they have entered so far have been shown explicitly. Ask them to add another box to the map and enter something about the character that they are able to figure out themselves based on these explicit traits. Demonstrate with a think-aloud:

    > I know that someone who loves to read probably reads a lot. A person who reads a lot gains information or learns from what he or she reads. A

person who knows lots of information is smart. So I know that Pony Boy is probably smart. I will put that in the box projecting out from "Loves to read."

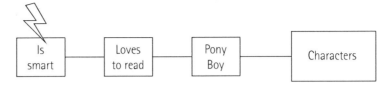

8. For homework, ask students to read the chapters of the book on which the portion of the movie they've seen is based and to continue making inferences about the characters.

9. In class the next day, discuss the character traits the students discovered and the inferences they made.

Assessment

Monitor the students' progress: Roam the room, stopping to mediate student understanding by answering questions and giving direction. The completed character maps are evidence of student understanding.

Advantages for English Language Learners

Even beginning English language learners gain some idea of the story by watching the movie. Meet with the English language learners and help them construct the graphic organizer. This will help them organize the information and make connections to their own previous knowledge and experience. Explaining the thinking involved in making an inference (metacognition) helps the students understand what you expect them to do.

Reading Boxes

This strategy, adapted from Lakeshore Learning's literature-based theme packets, also provides clues to understanding before students begin to read. It can be used with literacy as well as content-area instruction at all grade levels.

Making a reading box requires some thought and work ahead of time, but once you've made one, it can be used again and again. The first step is to assemble props or visuals related to the book, story, or article students will read. Then group them in a storage box of some kind, along with one copy of the text.

To use the reading box, gather students at a table or on the floor as a large group. Show the box to students and explain what it is. Briefly talk about the title, author, genre, topic, setting, and cultural background of the text, and give a short summary.

Next, take each prop out of the box, name the object, and explain its relevance to the story. Pass it around so students can touch it and look at it closely. Have students discuss the connections they make to the objects with a partner or with the whole group. Talking aloud in pairs (Kagan 1992) allows English language learners to voice their thoughts and practice speaking English in an unthreatening atmosphere.

Conduct the next part of the lesson like any other reading comprehension lesson, having students begin reading the text individually or in a literature circle. Work on specific grade-level reading skills and standards (predicting and confirming, for example).

──── **LESSON PLAN: READING *SADAKO* (COERR 1993)** ────

Grade Level: Fourth through sixth grades

English Language Learner Suitability: Beginning through advanced

Objective: Students will build background knowledge and vocabulary before reading *Sadako*. The lesson also will help students practice using prediction and confirmation as a reading comprehension strategy.

IRA/NCTE English Language Arts Standard 3: Students apply a wide range of strategies to comprehend, interpret, evaluate, and appreciate texts.

National TESOL Goal 2, Standard 2: To use English to achieve academically in all content areas. Students will use English to obtain, process, construct, and provide subject matter information in spoken and written form.

Curriculum Standard for the Social Studies, Middle Grades: Articulate the implications of cultural diversity, as well as cohesion, within and across groups.

Materials

Cardboard magazine storage box, decorated (with title, appropriate vocabulary, related pictures) and containing the following items:

- one copy of *Sadako*
- a rice-paper lantern
- origami cranes of various sizes
- a pair of chopsticks
- a track jersey

- a Japanese tea cup
- a stethoscope from a toy doctor kit
- a *National Geographic* photograph of a Japanese man and of the jacket he was wearing when the atomic bomb exploded (or a similar photograph from Hiroshima)
- a pad of small sticky notes

Procedure

1. Talk briefly about the book: title, author, genre, topic, setting, cultural background, and plot summary.
2. Show each prop to students and pass it around the group. Name each object and explain its relevance to the story and Japanese culture. Ask students, in pairs or as a whole group, to discuss the personal connections they make to the objects.
3. Have students, individually or in heterogeneous collaborative groups, read a set number of pages in the book. Ask them as they read to make predictions (the lesson presupposes students have been taught how to predict and confirm)—based on what you have shown and told them, their own personal knowledge, and the text—about what will happen next. Have them write each prediction on a sticky note and place it in the book at the point they make the prediction. This helps students understand the story better and keeps them reading to find out what happens next.
4. As they continue to read, have them mark any additional predictions with a sticky note, and also note any confirmations/denials of predictions (*Yeah! I was right! Oops! I was wrong!*).
5. After they finish the assigned reading, have students share their predictions, confirmations, and denials with you and their group members. Ask them to explain why they placed sticky notes in particular places.

Assessment

Roam among the students, checking to see that they are marking their predictions, confirmations, and denials with sticky notes and helping students individually as necessary.

═══ LESSON PLAN: EXPERIENCING THE CIVIL WAR ═══

Grade Level: Eighth grade

English Language Learner Suitability: Beginning through advanced

Objective: Students will research the life of either a Confederate or Union soldier using the resources in the reading box. Pretending to be that soldier, students will write letters home describing the job, the conditions and hardships they experience, how they deal with these hardships, and the geographical features of their location. Students will include five new vocabulary words that relate to life as a soldier.

IRA/NCTE English Language Arts Standard 7: Students conduct research on issues and interests by generating ideas and questions and by posing problems. They gather, evaluate, and synthesize data from a variety of sources (e.g., print and nonprint texts, artifacts, people) to communicate their discoveries in ways that suit their purpose and audience.

National TESOL Goal 2, Grades 4–8: To use English to achieve academically in all content areas. Students will use appropriate learning strategies to construct and apply academic knowledge.

Standards in History for Grades 5–12, Era 5—Civil War and Reconstruction. Standard 1: The causes of the Civil War. Standard 2: The course and character of the Civil War and its effects on the American people.

Materials

- Two Civil War reading boxes. Some of the contents may seem childish to use with adolescents, but they help develop basic vocabulary (*soldier, canon, wheels, rifle, charge, march, gear, cabin*) that beginning English language learners do not know.

Union Box	Confederate Box
• toy figure of Lincoln	• toy figure of Jefferson Davis
• toy Union soldiers	• toy Confederate soldiers
• small glass lantern	• small glass lantern
• illustrated book, *Lincoln's Gettysburg Address* (Scholastic)	• illustrated book, *Lincoln's Gettysburg Address* (Scholastic)
• illustrated timeline of Civil War	• illustrated timeline of Civil War
• map of Union and Confederate states	• map of Union and Confederate states
• illustrated article of Northern life	• Confederate culture article
• army camp life article	• army camp life article
• black volunteers article	• black volunteers article
• food and rations piece	• food and rations piece
• camp lingo (vocabulary)	• camp lingo (vocabulary)
• military medical care insert	• military medical care insert
• photographs of Union cavalry artifacts	• photographs of Confederate cavalry artifacts
• sample journal entries/letters home	• sample journal entries/letters home

Procedure

1. Have students use one of the reading boxes to gather background information on either a Confederate or Union soldier.
2. When students find a fact they want to use, ask them to summarize it in three essential words. Then have them write the fact on an index card in their own words, incorporating the three words.
3. Have each student use his or her note cards to write a rough draft of a letter, pretending to be a soldier writing home.
4. Ask students, in pairs, to read the rough drafts of their letters to each other, checking to see whether they have included answers to the following questions.

Civil War Project

Essential Questions for Revising Your First Draft

(Adapted from Bearse and Harutunian 2005)

Job:
- What do you like and dislike?
- What is the hardest part?
- What is the easiest part?
- Do you have responsibilities you are afraid of?
- Which weapons do you use, and how have they helped you in battle?

Camp life:
- When you are not fighting, what do you like to do with the other soldiers?
- What is most boring about serving in the army?
- What do you like or dislike about the food?

Physical challenges on the battlefield:
- Look around the battlefield: What do you see, taste, hear, smell, feel?
- Are any of your friends nearby? Is anyone in pain? dead? frightened?
- Do you have nightmares about things that have happened in battle?
- Have you been thinking about anyone or anything to give you the will to stay alive?

What you miss:
- What do you need or miss? (food? family? friends? other things?)
- How do you feel emotionally? What do you want to tell the person you are writing to make yourself feel better?

Including information about their jobs, camp life, physical challenges, and feelings requires students to add details; their letters become more interesting.

5. Ask students to look up three words in a thesaurus to improve their descriptive language. For example, if they wrote, "The battlefield was big," they might look up *big* and change it to *enormous*.
6. Teach a minilesson on similes and ask students to find two things in their letters about which they can create a simile.
7. Have each student submit the final version of his or her letter.

Advantages for English Language Learners

For beginning and intermediate levels, use the preview-view-review strategy (Freeman and Freeman 2004). *Preview* the lesson in the primary language of the students. (If a primary language speaker is not available, have the students look through a trade book or text in the primary language.) Conduct the lesson in English (*view*), and afterward clear up any misconceptions students may have (*review*). If you are not bilingual and don't have a bilingual instructional assistant, have students work in pairs, teaming a bilingual English learner with a greater understanding of English with a bilingual English learner just beginning to speak and understand English. The more proficient reader can read the material aloud, and the students can discuss the reading in their first language.

Manipulatives

Using manipulatives helps students enhance their mental images as they solve problems or try to understand a new concept. Manipulatives support students' understanding of abstract concepts in a concrete way and appeal to the bodily/kinesthetic intelligence (Gardner 1983).

Manipulatives are often used in math and science instruction but can be used in many other subject areas and at all grade levels. For example, interlocking block manipulatives can be used to teach phonics and word recognition. Students manipulate the blocks as they match the beginning sounds of words to pictures, combine beginning chunks with ending chunks, and move word blocks to form sentences. See the next page for an example.

| B |
| tr | ain | | I love to read. |

Many math programs come with containers of colored blocks, geometric shapes, plastic teddy bears, and the like that students move around or manipulate during math lessons. Teachers use these items to teach such concepts as multiplication, measurement, fractional parts, and geometry in a concrete, hands-on way. For example, to understand multiplication, students can represent the problem 5×4 with plastic squares, creating five groups with four blocks in each (an *array*) and then counting all the blocks to find the answer of twenty.

LESSON PLAN:
CREATING A REMEMBRANCE QUILT

Grade Level: Second grade

English Language Learner Suitability: Beginning through advanced

Objective: Students will learn about geometric shapes by recreating shapes on geoboards during a unit on family traditions.

IRA/NCTE English Language Arts Standard 12: Students use spoken, written, and visual language to accomplish their own purposes (e.g., for enjoyment, learning, persuasion, and the exchange of information).

National TESOL Goal 2, Standard 2: To use English to achieve academically in all content areas. Students will use English to obtain, process, construct, and provide subject matter information in spoken and written form.

Curriculum Standards for Social Studies—Time, Continuity, and Change: Demonstrate an understanding that different people may describe the same event or situation in diverse ways, citing reasons for the differences in views.

Materials

- Tangrams in different colors and shapes
- Geometric shapes made out of different colors of construction paper

- Books on quilts, for example:
  - *The Tortilla Quilt* (Tenorio-Coscarelli 1996)
  - *The Whispering Cloth* (Shea 1995)
  - *Shota and the Star Quilt* (Bateson-Hill 1998)

Overview

Students manipulate geometric shapes to form patterns for quilt squares. Then they write about things the shapes remind them of relative to their native countries. Students then work in collaborative groups to create collective "remembrance quilts" similar to the ones in the books they have read or heard read to them during the unit. Each quilt square celebrates something relative to a student's heritage.

Procedure

1. Read several books on quilts aloud to the class. The books should reflect the ethnicities of the students. For example, if the class has Native American students, *Shota and the Star Quilt* is a good choice.
2. Introduce the geometric shapes to form a picture (tangrams).
3. Have students, in groups, manipulate the tangrams and create patterns or pictures.
4. Ask students to discuss these patterns or pictures and decide on the shapes and colors they will use to create their individual patterns or picture for the memory quilts.
5. Students use construction paper to make their individual patterns or pictures.
6. Have students, working in collaborative groups, use textbooks, trade books, and the Internet to make connections between the shapes they have created and their family heritage.
7. Have students write about what their shapes or pictures remind them of relative to their homelands or ancestors.
8. Students glue their patterns or pictures to their construction paper squares.
9. Ask each group to create a memory quilt from the members' shapes.
10. Have the groups present their projects to the class. Mediate the students' observations and comments.

Assessment

Informally evaluate the groups as they present their quilts to the class and explain the relevance of each square to the theme of family traditions.

Advantages for English Language Learners

This lesson has several advantages for English language learners. It is a hands-on math lesson that includes students' backgrounds or cultural heritages. This engages the students in the lesson. They are able to understand geometric shapes through manipulating them into the desired patterns or pictures.

Collaborative Grouping

Studies have shown that cooperative learning is useful for increasing achievement in addition to encouraging student involvement and enhancing motivation (Polloway, Patton, and Serna 2001). A particularly relevant finding, especially for classrooms comprising diverse students, is that there is a tremendous increase in positive personal interactions among students of different ethnic backgrounds as a result of working collaboratively (Brandt 1990).

When working and solving problems together (rather than just engaging in open discussion), students use spoken language as they try to understand the problem they are solving or the investigation they are completing. By restating what they remember from the teacher's lecture or lesson and discussing their understanding with others, students gain a more in-depth understanding of the lesson content and its academic language. Students have to think and listen to one another.

Teachers sometimes are reluctant to allow students to converse because they see it as a temptation to engage in off-task behavior. Explain that the goal is not only to complete an assignment but also to count on one another to get the job done, and train students in the specific behavior essential to working collaboratively. When you use cooperative structures such as think-pair-share (Kagan 1994), inside/outside circle (Baloche 1998, Kagan 1992), or four corners (Kagan 1990), make sure students understand the intent of working together and the procedures involved in the structure.

Your role as the teacher is critical. You cannot sit passively and observe, nor be intrusive and take control of the discussions. Walk from group to group listening to and watching student interactions. Mediate as necessary to keep students on task and moving forward. Don't succumb to the temptation to catch up on paperwork when students appear to be involved and working productively. Students will not work together seriously unless they know that you value working collaboratively and will hold them accountable for what takes place within the group.

The following lesson plan is a game that shows how a teacher can use collaborative group work in instruction.

——————— LESSON PLAN: COMMUNITY GAMES ———————

Grade Level: Second grade

English Language Learner Suitability: Beginning through advanced

Objective: Students, in groups of four, will learn the importance of working together as a community by creating the longest line of items placed together on a piece of butcher paper. Students will discover ways to cover the longest distance; for example, unbending the paper clips will lengthen the line of items.

IRA/NCTE English Language Arts Standard 11: Students participate as knowledgeable, reflective, creative, and critical members of a variety of literacy communities.

National TESOL Goal 1, Standard 1: To use English to communicate in social settings. Students will use English to participate in social interactions.

Curriculum Standards for Social Studies: Identify and describe ways family, groups, and community influence the individual's daily life and personal choices. Discuss the importance of public virtue and the role of citizens, including how to participate in a classroom, in the community, and in civic life.

Materials (for each group of four)

- A plastic bag containing one pencil, four paper clips, and a six-inch length of yarn
- A strip of blank butcher paper
- A ruler for each group

Procedure

1. Divide students into groups of four.
2. Give each group a bag of materials.
3. Ask them, as a group, to line up all the items on the piece of butcher paper against the ruler, in any way that they wish, in an attempt to cover the longest distance.
4. Measure each group's line of items and identify the winning group.

5. Hold a class discussion about what was helpful and unhelpful in the group interactions, relating the activity to the workings of a community.

6. Have students write for five minutes about how they worked as a community to
complete the task.

Assessment

Read and evaluate the writing students have done.

Advantages for English Language Learners

This lesson works well for all levels of English learners. Beginners do not need to use
language to be part of the group. They can observe what others are trying to do and
participate. They understand English in a receptive way, and other students speak as
they touch and manipulate the concrete items. Through conversation, intermediate
and advanced learners are developing English language skills, as well as the idea of
community. Students work collaboratively to complete the task.

Moving to Learn

People communicate with one another in many ways. Generally we think of
language as our primary means of communication, but that is not always the
case. Trial lawyers often hire experts to read the body language of prospective
jurors as they answer questions meant to determine their suitability. Our gestures, facial expressions, body posture, and overall movement add to our communication. More is communicated nonverbally than most teachers realize.
Teachers can capitalize on this by using nonverbal cues to convey meaning to
English learners.

An important way students learn is through their bodily/kinesthetic intelligence (Gardner 1983)—by touching things during hands-on activities, by
using their bodies, by moving to learn. Gardner says:

> The brain learns best and retains most when the organism is actively
> involved in exploring physical sites and materials and asking questions to
> which it actually craves answers. Merely passive experiences tend to attenu-
> ate and have little lasting impact. (1999, 82)

Classroom activities that provide opportunities for moving to learn include playing games (charades, for example), dancing, acting or role-playing, chanting, drawing pictures, and working in small groups (building models, making a display or diorama, making or showing a video, or performing an experiment). When teachers contextualize learning through movement, students engage and remember their learning.

The following lesson plan is an example of using movement to learn the concept of classification.

LESSON PLAN: CLASSIFICATION

Grade Level: Second and third grades

English Language Learner Suitability: Beginning through advanced

Objective: Students will organize themselves into groups based on similarities.

IRA/NCTE English Language Arts Standard 12: Students use spoken, written, and visual language to accomplish their own purposes (e.g., for learning, enjoyment, persuasion, and the exchange of information).

National TESOL Goal 2, Standard 1: To use English to achieve academically in all content areas. Students will use English to interact in the classroom.

Materials

None.

Procedure

1. Ask students to count off from one to four and form four groups: ones, twos, threes, and fours. (This cooperative structure is known as four corners; see Kagan 1990.)
2. Each group then divides into subgroups based on characteristics the members decide they have in common: gender, height (tall, medium height, short), month of birth, color of clothing, and so on.
3. Conduct several rounds of subgroupings using different defining characteristics.
4. As each group reveals its subgroups to the class, write the defining characteristics on the board.
5. Ask students, in pairs, to explain to each other what classifying means and why being able to do it is important.

Assessment

Determine whether each group has created subgroups according to the common characteristics the members identified.

Advantages for English Language Learners

This lesson asks students to use higher level thinking skills through classifying even though they are not very familiar with speaking and understanding English. They are asked to physically move, which means they show their understanding in a nonverbal way. This allows for equity of participation. Again, they show their understanding and participate in the group project because it is hands-on and highly contextualized.

Final Thoughts

It is our hope that teachers will use the contextualization scaffold to replace instruction that does not engage their English learners in learning and to alleviate instruction that is too difficult to understand. As we have stated, there are many ways to contextualize a lesson. Every lesson should contain contextualization in some form in order to support students with different learning styles as well as English learners.

The Chapter in a Nutshell

Scaffold: Contextualizing

Teachers organize visual and physical information in a way that enables all students to make sense of a lesson.

Appropriate grade levels: K–2, 3–5, 6–8

Strategies

Visuals (props, real objects, photographs, videos)

Manipulatives

Collaborative grouping

Moving to learn

Content area

- Social studies
- Math
- Science
- Reading/language arts
- Reading
- Writing
- Listening
- Speaking
- Language processes

How is it done?

Visuals: Teachers use photographs, drawings, pictures, big books, picture books, children's artwork, videos, models, artifacts, and props to add informational clues to lessons. Students connect the terminology to the visual images.

Manipulatives: Teachers help students understand abstract concepts by demonstrating them with concrete objects.

Collaborative grouping: Teachers encourage students to share ideas by talking together. Students work together in small, heterogeneous groups to solve a content-related problem, work on a project, or complete an assignment.

Moving to learn: Teachers engage students in physical activity in which learning is the byproduct, not the focus.

Why is the scaffold important to use?

Using props and visuals builds English language skills and background knowledge, increases understanding, and helps students access knowledge and experiences they already have. The lesson becomes more interesting and enjoyable.

Manipulatives offer a mode of kinesthetic learning. Students develop cognitively by manipulating objects to demonstrate the ideas they represent.

In collaborative grouping, more students talk and participate in the lesson than in a whole-group setting. Students ask real, authentic questions and respond to others. Talking while problem solving helps contextualize the language, making it more understandable. It promotes second language acquisition and academic vocabulary.

Learning activities that involve movement help students remember what they are learning.

Thinking About Thinking

Develop a Mental Framework

The most powerful thing we can teach is strategic knowledge—a knowledge of the procedures people use to learn, to think, to read, and to write. The most effective way to introduce students to how to use these tools is to model them in the contexts of meaningful tasks and then to assist students in their own use of these strategies.

——JEFFREY WILHELM

When teachers worry excessively about fitting in all the instruction they are expected to cover, opportunities to work with new ideas do not materialize. Teachers intuitively know students learn more and remember longer when given multiple opportunities to work with new ideas. In many school districts, the number of standards teachers are expected to teach in a given school year is a physical impossibility. Wiggins and McTighe (1998) suggest that material worth teaching:

1. has value beyond the classroom
2. is at the heart of the related discipline
3. comprises ideas that are abstract or often misunderstood
4. is potentially engaging

Applying these criteria helps teachers and grade-level teams choose judiciously the standards they will cover in a year, relieving undue pressure and creating more time for students to work with ideas. The point is for students to learn to remember, not just learn for a test.

Strategies to help people learn go back to the very origins of education. While there is still much we do not know, it is clear that knowledge has to be actively acquired by the student and that knowledge the student already has influences new knowledge. It is also clear that individuals learn in a number of ways. Rote memorization is certainly one, but very little information gained that way is retained for any length of time. Students can also learn meaningfully, integrating new concepts into previously acquired knowledge (Novak 2002).

Two important concepts related to this kind of learning are schema and metacognition. A *schema* is the mental framework by which we organize concepts; *metacognition* is being aware of our own thinking processes. Teachers encourage schema building and metacognition by:

- helping students build background knowledge and understanding
- helping students access the background knowledge they already have and use it as a bridge to new learning
- helping students become consciously aware of their thinking processes and the strategies they use to accomplish tasks

Students' background knowledge about content they are learning and the mental connections they make, along with their personal, cultural, and academic experiences, influence their success in learning new material. English language learners must be explicitly taught strategies for becoming aware of their own thinking and how to apply those strategies to other learning situations.

Building Background Knowledge

Helping students develop background knowledge on a topic involves teaching students to access the information they have stored in memory and add information that is not there. When students do not have the background knowledge necessary to engage with a particular lesson, their motivation declines as the lesson progresses and they are left behind. Teachers need to help them build the necessary schema—the essential mental framework needed to understand the lesson—and make them aware that they need to use that information in school tasks.

What can a teacher do when it is evident students do not have background knowledge? Introducing a variety of materials, leading whole- and small-group discussions, showing video clips, reading aloud, and helping students bridge what they know with new information are all ways to help students understand and store new information in their long-term memories. Students can then organize these pieces of information and increase the number of connections they can make.

———— **LESSON PLAN: BLACK CULTURE TEA PARTY** ————

Grade Level: Fourth through sixth grade

English Language Learner Suitability: Beginning through advanced

Objective: The lesson will prepare students to understand *Grandpa, Is Everything Black Bad?* by making sense of phrases from the book and posing questions, thus promoting an understanding of African American heritage.

IRA/NCTE English Language Arts Standard 1: Students read a wide range of print and nonprint texts to build an understanding of texts, of themselves, and of the cultures of the United States.

National TESOL Goal 2, Standard 1: To use English to achieve academically in all content areas. Students will use English to interact in the classroom.

Curriculum Standards for Social Studies: Explain and give examples of how language, literature, the arts, architecture, other artifacts, traditions, beliefs, values, and behaviors contribute to the development and transmission of culture.

Materials

- A copy of *Grandpa, Is Everything Black Bad?* (Holman 1999)
- A piece of paper containing a phrase from the text for each student in the class

Overview

Students share small strips of text with one another before reading *Grandpa, Is Everything Black Bad?*, a story about a young African American boy who is coming to terms with his African heritage. This background helps students of any ethnicity relate to the boy's problem and sets the stage for lessons to come.

Procedure

1. Retype the first four or five pages of the book in a large font, double- or triple-spaced. Cut up the text into meaningful bits of information, numbered in sequential order, like this:

   - It's dark, *black* and scary
   - in my bedroom at night.
   - So I hide
   - under the covers
   - when Dad turns out the light.
   - I like watching TV,
   - but sometimes I'm sad,
   - because most white things are good,
   - and most *black* things are bad. (from pages 1 and 2)

   - People wear the color *black*,
   - when somebody dies.
   - They look very sad
   - and have tears in their eyes.
   - "Grandpa, is everything *black* bad?" (from pages 3 and 4).

   If you wish, you can glue each strip onto an index card and laminate it.

2. Hand out a numbered slip of paper (or card) to each student.
3. Have each student begin reading his or her line to every other student.

4. Ask the students to freeze. Ask them to predict what they think the book will be about. Ask them to think about the significance of the color black in the story.

5. Have the students form a circle in the order of the numbers on their slips of paper. Then ask them to read their phrases aloud, in order.

6. Now that all the students have heard the beginning of the book, ask them to revise their predictions and talk about aspects of African American culture.

Assessment

Listen to students as they predict and as they pose questions.

Advantages for English Language Learners

Choose the phrases English language learners receive based on their reading ability, and help them practice their phrases before they read them to the other students. This strategy enables students to make sense of the text with the support of other students. This lesson allows English learners more time to process information, and in so doing they make stronger text-to-self connections.

Bridging Past Learning and New Learning

When students already have the mental framework for a lesson in place, teachers must help them connect their prior knowledge and experiences to the new information. This can be accomplished by questioning, charting, journaling, or making direct statements that help students see the bigger picture: "What did we learn yesterday about such and such?" "Let's take a look at what we charted last week." The point is to make sure all students have enough understanding to begin the new lesson.

Rumelhart (1980) suggests that for learning to occur, new information has to be integrated with what the learner already knows—that is, linked to students' personal, cultural, and academic experiences. Teachers often assume that all students in the class have the same background experiences because they all live in America and are about the same age. The reality is that students' backgrounds can vary dramatically. For example, in a writing assignment teachers may ask students to imagine what it feels like to trudge through freshly fallen snow or sit on the beach looking at the ocean. English language learners who do not have these experiences, who do not have background knowledge about snow or the beach, will not do well on the assignment because they cannot write about experiences and knowledge they do not have.

In her classroom, Denise needs to connect to the cultural experiences of her Hmong students in order for them to learn. For example, if she were to talk about having a birthday party, celebrating Christmas, or going on vacation as a possible subject for a story, her Hmong students would not be able to make the appropriate connections. So she refers to Hmong cultural experiences as well: family reunions, fishing and hunting, and the seasons and agriculture.

Many times students from culturally diverse backgrounds have a mental framework or visual patterns different from a text's intended audience. English language learners do have experiences and knowledge, but they may differ from the experiences and knowledge other students have and value in school. It is easy for teachers to assume that students who do not understand what they read are ignorant when, in fact, they may have gaps in their learning and/or have developed different schemas. It is up to the teacher to fill the gaps or build bridges to appropriate background knowledge so English language learners can participate fully.

An informative area of teacher research is cognitive processing—how people store and retrieve information. This research reaffirms the importance of helping students develop a "well-connected body of accessible knowledge" (Rosenshine 1997, 217). By making connections between prior information and ideas and what they are currently studying, students can use higher-order thinking skills and see where ideas fit in the larger scheme of things, thus attributing a deeper meaning to their schoolwork.

Cognitive psychologists George Lakoff and Mark Johnson (1980) have studied memory processes and offer some new information on reading, writing, and memory. They have examined metaphor as a tool for thinking and found that people regularly think and converse in metaphor. They cite as examples common metaphors related to war: "His criticisms were *right on target*. He *shot down* all my arguments." Metaphors rely on our ability to bridge the new with the known—our ability to use schema. A difficult concept to teach and understand becomes easier when we accept metaphor as a natural extension of the way children think and make sense of their world (Cunningham and Shagoury 2005).

───── LESSON PLAN: USING METAPHOR ─────

Grade Level: Kindergarten through second grade

English Language Learner Suitability: Beginning through advanced

Objective: This lesson (adapted from Cunningham and Shagoury 2005, 42–67) uses metaphor and a nonfiction book to explain the concept of courage. Children will recognize the similarity between the actions of a tree frog and their own actions.

IRA/NCTE English Language Arts Standard 2: Students read a wide range of literature from many periods in many genres to build an understanding of the many dimensions (e.g., philosophical, ethical, aesthetic) of human experience.

National TESOL Goal 1, Standard 2: To use English to communicate in social settings. Students will interact in, through, and with spoken and written English for personal expression and enjoyment.

Materials

- The picture book *Red-Eyed Tree Frog* (Cowley 1999)
- Twelve-inch-by-eighteen-inch drawing paper, folded in half
- Crayons, markers, or colored pencils

Overview

This lesson shows how teachers can take a difficult concept for kindergartners—courage—and have children understand the relationship between two unlike ideas, the similarity between the actions of a tree frog and their own actions. Students are asked to bridge the new with the known.

Procedure

1. Read *Red-Eyed Tree Frog* aloud as the students follow along, looking at the pictures. Afterward, emphasize that the tree frog leads a dangerous life. Every day is a struggle to elude its predators.
2. On a subsequent day, reread the book, asking students to pick an action of a tree frog that they will demonstrate. Some English language learners struggle to find

words to convey what they know. Movement allows them to make sense of what they read or listen to.

3. Have students share their re-creations of frog actions with the class.
4. Focus the students' attention on the actions that show the red-eyed frog demonstrating courage.
5. Ask each student to draw two pictures on a piece of folded paper: on one half, one of the frog's daily courageous acts; on the other, a daily courageous act the student performs.
6. Have each student tell about the two pictures and describe the relationship between the two unlike situations, thus introducing the class to the concept of metaphor.

Assessment

Observe the students to be sure they understand and respond to the movement activity.

Listen to the students explain the relationship between their two drawings and/or evaluate their drawings.

Advantages for English Language Learners

Students show their understanding through actions. Allow them to draw the metaphoric concept without having to explain it orally. This lesson is an example of a more challenging curricula for English learners.

Metacognition

Students tend to rely on the only learning strategy they may know—memorization—to help them succeed in school. Studies show that this is not how we learn, much less how we remember what we have learned. Teachers need to explicitly teach students strategies for learning. This gives them a "heads up" on how to learn and how to use what they know.

Metacognitive strategies encourage students to reflect on their assignments or completed tasks, such as presenting a project, reading a book, or writing the final draft of a paper. Teachers can provide opportunities for students to use and develop metacognitive skills by asking, "What did you gain from this experience?" or "What would you do differently if you could return to the project?"

Ed Thurston uses a test-debriefing strategy adapted from Weimer (2002). After giving students a unit exam he has created himself, Ed asks them to look carefully at the questions they missed. Then the test debriefing continues with these steps.

1. Ed identifies which questions from the test were based on his class lectures and activities and which were based on the assigned course readings. Which type of question did they miss most often? Were the answers explicitly stated or did they need to make inferences?

2. Students look through their tests and figure out why they missed each question. Did they misread it? Did they not understand it? Did they read into the question information that was not there? Did they not know the answer? Students get a picture of their test-taking skills.

3. Students do a think-pair-share (Kagan 1994). In pairs, students share what they have discovered about their test-taking skills. Each pair of students then shares this same information with another pair of students. This time they work together to place the errors into categories, thus discovering whether, for example, they need to study the content more than the assigned course readings or focus on not reading more into a question than it is explicitly asking.

4. Ed asks students to begin to internalize their learning by writing in their metacognitive journal. One side of a divided page is headed, "What I learned," the other, "How I came to learn it."

As a result of this strategy, students become consciously aware of how to prepare for and take tests successfully. They gain control over their thinking about tests and test-taking strategies and can use their strategies to improve their own test-taking skills. It may appear to some students that "some people are just good test takers" and "some are not." They do not realize that reviewing lecture notes and course readings as well as learning strategies about how to answer questions all come into play. Being a successful test taker is not something left to chance. It is a skill that can be learned.

For any metacognitive strategy to be effective, students must:

1. understand the strategy
2. understand why they need to know it and why it will benefit them
3. be able to think through the strategy process aloud or voice the strategy in their mind
4. see examples of the strategy in use
5. know when and where it is appropriate to use the strategy
6. be able to monitor themselves (Is the strategy working? What should be done if it does not work?)

Graphic Organizers

One way teachers can help students make connections and internalize concepts is through graphic organizers. Graphic organizers are concrete, pictorial ways of constructing knowledge and organizing information. They enable students to build, access, bridge, and interconnect what they have learned by converting and compressing a lot of seemingly disjointed information into a structured, simple-to-read graphic display.

Visual diagrams convey complicated information simply. They are critical to student understanding, whether students create them or they are presented as part of the teacher's instruction. Since the words on the organizer are few, students just beginning to learn English can participate in the higher-level thinking required to create it.

There are different types of graphic organizers for different ways of processing information. They can be used to help students solve problems, make decisions, study, plan research, and brainstorm. There are four basic structures (Griffin and Tulbert 1995).

1. A *hierarchical* structure delineates a concept and its subconcepts.

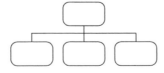

This structure can be used to explore topics that have different levels. It is more commonly referred to as a *tree diagram* and can be used for lineage studies and charting family members.

2. A *sequential* structure delineates events in the order in which they appear or occur (a time line, for example).

3. A *conceptual* structure delineates relationships between different concepts and includes supporting facts and characteristics (and sometimes examples).

Examples of this kind of graphic organizer are the Venn diagram and a web.

4. A *cyclical* structure delineates events or processes that repeat.

Teachers can use modified forms of these four graphic organizers depending on the objective of the lesson.

Figure 4–1 shows how ideas are linked from general to specific, letting students see how new learning interconnects with what they have already learned about the desert.

Let's deconstruct how a teacher and his students created this organizer.

1. They defined the topic. What did they want to know? In this case, they wanted to learn about important desert concepts.

2. They identified and listed the most important general ideas about the topic: "extreme heat," "extreme dryness," "cold nights," "home to living things."

3. They listed general ideas first, then more specific aspects of those ideas. For example, the general idea "home to living things" connects to "plants" and "animals."

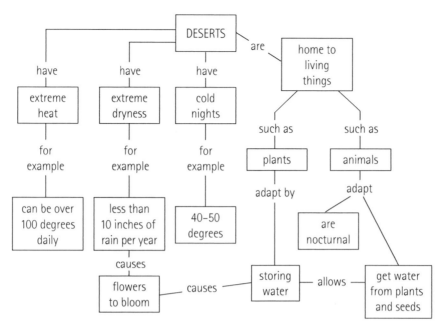

Figure 4.1 Variation of a Hierarchical–Conceptual Graphic Organizer

4. They added links to ideas that are still more specific, using words and phrases that describe relationships. For example, "animals" is linked to "are nocturnal" with the word "adapt," capturing the idea that becoming nocturnal is how animals have adapted to the desert environment.

They added horizontal cross-links between ideas. For example, at the bottom of the diagram, they linked "flowers to bloom," "storing water," and "get water from plants and seeds" to capture the idea that the small amount of rain causes flowers to bloom and plants to store water, which is how animals can get water to survive. (Adapted from Novak and Gowin 1984.) Note that most graphic organizers do not have linking words or cross-links. In this case, both are essential to clarify ideas.

Students need guided practice while learning how to develop graphic organizers. They are a wonderful tool for understanding, but only if students are able to create them themselves. Creating a graphic organizer requires the following thinking: identify the relationships between the concepts; determine what each relationship means; pick out the most important information; and place each item of information in the proper hierarchy.

The Chapter in a Nutshell

Scaffold: Building schema and metacognition

Teachers help students create frameworks for understanding and consciously think about their own thinking.

Appropriate grade levels: K–2 (modified), 3–5, 6–8

Strategies

Tea party

Metaphor lesson

Test debriefing

Content area

- Social studies
- Math
- Science
- Reading/language arts
- Reading
- Writing
- Listening
- Speaking
- Language processes

How is it done?

Tea party: Students prepare for a lesson by discussing what they already know about a topic.

Metaphor lesson: Students link new understanding to background knowledge and experiences by discovering how two unrelated experiences are similar.

Test debriefing: Students reflect on their test preparation and test-taking skills and make improvements based on what they discover.

Why is the scaffold important to use?

It fills in gaps in the learning and understanding of English language learners and helps them be conscious of their own role in their learning.

Reframing Information

5

First of all, when you are trying to present new materials, you cannot expect them to be grasped immediately. If they are, in fact, the understanding had probably been present all along. One must approach the issue in many different ways over a significant period of time if there is to be any hope of assimilation.

— HOWARD GARDNER, *FRAMES OF MIND*

Howard Gardner, in the epigraph above, is telling us what teachers know from experience—students do not instantly learn what the teacher teaches. They need time to process new information. To that end, instructors present material in different ways over time. Reframing information (Walqui 2003) allows the teacher to do just this—have students revisit information or text and interpret it in a different way. This scaffold encourages higher-level thinking (Bloom 1956) and understanding because it lets students show their comprehension of written material by creating engaging and innovative versions of it. Examples of these kinds of strategies include readers theatre, miniperformances, poetry, murals, and tableaus.

Readers Theatre

Readers theatre is "the oral presentation of drama, prose, or poetry by two or more readers" (McCaslin 1990, 263). Students read or listen to a story or informational text, take the main ideas they discover, and write a script revealing those ideas; alternatively they may use a script the teacher provides. In traditional readers theatre the script is not memorized but read, and there is no scenery, makeup, or props. However, incorporating music, lighting, small props, and gestures is a way to clarify meaning for English language learners and provide them with greater understanding. We know from brain research and the theory of multiple intelligences that physical movement and gestures help students remember what they learn (Jensen 1998).

Since readers theatre is performed for an audience, there is a real reason for students to read and reread the script until it can be performed fluently—until they sound as if they are talking. The teacher models how to read with expression, how different intonations and reading rates affect meaning, and how important reading and rereading are. Readers theatre also lets teachers monitor students' reading comprehension because students retell the story as they practice the scripts. This teacher monitoring, intervening when necessary, is important, especially for English language learners; students should not be rehearsing lines that have no meaning for them. Ideally, teachers will discover and meet their students' individual needs, assigning parts based on every English language learner's current facility with spoken English.

Readers theatre is traditionally created from narratives and stories, but grade-level standards now recommend an increased amount of expository text. Teachers are therefore including more nonfiction text in their language arts lessons, and readers theatre is one way to do this seamlessly. For example, the script *The Water Cycle*, available on the Enchanted Learning website (www.enchantedlearning.com), helps listeners create a mental image of condensation. Here's an excerpt:

WATER VAPOR 1: What's water vapor?

WATER VAPOR 2: It's water, but it's a gas. You've evaporated and turned into a gas and so have I. Let's fly up high!

WATER VAPOR 1: I feel like joining the others and forming a crowd.

WATER VAPOR 2: I think you mean a cloud, not a crowd. Okay, let's condense.

WATER VAPOR 1: What does that mean?

WATER VAPOR 2: Condensing means that we'll change back into a liquid (water, of course). Then we'll be part of a cloud.

Sometimes teachers of underperforming students feel pressured to improve test scores and begin focusing on reading, writing, and math to the exclusion of social studies and science. Integrating content information into reading lessons allows teachers to include science and social studies in their daily teaching while still focusing on English language development and English language arts. Students are reading and writing but are doing so about science and social studies instead of just literature.

Miniperformances

A type of modified readers theatre for younger students unable to read a script is the *miniperformance* (Morado, Koenig, and Wilson 1999). In this strategy, kindergartners and first and second graders listen to a story and then perform it, using their imagination to create improvised movement and dialogue. The teacher serves as the narrator and provides more elaborate props and sets than are usually used in readers theatre. This strategy helps students understand the skills of determining a sequence, relating cause and effect, and identifying a story's problem or moral.

Without giving it much thought teachers tend to choose more widely known and readily available European folktales. However, folktales are found in all cultures of the world and provide a common foundation for learning about the behavior, attitudes, and values of people (Crawford 1993).

--------------- **LESSON PLAN: THE FIRST FARMER** ---------------

Grade Level: First grade

English Language Learner Suitability: Beginning through advanced

Objective: Students will dramatize a folktale by creating original dialogue, in the process identifying the characters, setting, important events, and moral of the story.

IRA/NCTE English Language Arts Standard 6: Students apply knowledge of language structure, language conventions (e.g., spelling and punctuation), media techniques, figurative language, and genre to create, critique, and discuss print and nonprint texts.

IRA/NCTE English Language Arts Standard 9: Students develop an understanding and respect for diversity in language use, patterns, and dialects across cultures, ethnic groups, geographic regions, and social roles.

National TESOL Goal 2, Standard 1: To use English to achieve academically in all content areas. Students will use English to interact in the classroom.

Curriculum Standards for Social Studies: Explore and describe similarities and differences in the ways groups, societies, and cultures address similar human needs and concerns.

Materials

- A copy of *Tub Qoob Tub Loo, Farmer Boy* (Matthews 1994)
- Construction paper, tagboard, paints, markers, and old rulers (to glue masks to) for making props and a set

Overview

Since many of Denise's students are Hmong, she uses an authentic Hmong folktale, *The First Farmer*, to interest and value her learners and to access their background knowledge (see Chapter 4). This folktale explains what hard work it is to cultivate different kinds of crops and spend long days working in the fields. Many of Denise's students have heard the story before at home. The students are excited about making the plants and animals in the story come to life through their own imaginations and dialogue; they need very little assistance in making their character masks and props.

Procedure

1. First, read the story aloud. Identify and discuss the characters, the setting, and the main events. This may take several days.
2. Create a list of characters, and let the students choose their parts (narrator, two or three corn plants, two or three weeds, the tiger, the wildcat, the mouse, the cow, the wolf, the chicken, and the farmer). Pairs of students may be assigned a single part.
3. Familiarize the students with their playing area.
4. Reread the story, telling the students to pay attention to their chosen roles. Students need to understand their characters in order to know what to say in the enactment.

5. Ask students to decide what their character will say, and create a script as they tell you. This can be done in parts: beginning, middle, and end.

6. Have students practice their parts individually, adding actions and movement and gathering props. Then let them practice sections (beginning, middle, and end) as a group.

7. Remind students to speak in loud voices and be clear about what they are saying.

8. Have students present the entire miniperformance to an audience.

Assessment

Monitor the students individually as they prepare and practice the presentation, checking for understanding of their character and the setting, main idea, and moral of the story.

Advantages for English Language Learners

Students who are at beginning levels of English acquisition can pair up with another student in the same role. There are parts for many animals, and animal sounds can be made instead of words.

Poetry

Poetry is a major writing genre, and poetry selections consistently appear on today's standardized tests. Students need to know the elements of poetry as well as how to interpret it. Sometimes teachers do not feel comfortable teaching poetry and thus neglect it. Poetry can reframe nonfiction text much the same way readers theatre does. It is a great way to integrate science and social studies into lessons on English language arts and English language development.

Students need a basic understanding of poetry in order to benefit from this strategy. Here are the essential elements, which they can pick up from listening to and/or writing poetry in connection with some accompanying instruction.

Poems have *stanzas*—groups of lines.

Poems have *patterns of language*: rhythm, metaphor, assonance, alliteration, and rhyme.

A poem can:

- express a feeling
- tell a story
- describe something common or uncommon
- use imagery to create pictures with words

LESSON PLAN: BREATHE IN, BREATHE OUT

Grade Level: Fifth grade

English Language Learner Suitability: Beginning through advanced

Objective: Students, through poetry they write themselves, will explain how oxygen and carbon dioxide are exchanged in the lungs. In particular, the poems will use repeated words as a tool to convey meaning.

IRA/NCTE English Language Arts Standard 6: Students apply knowledge of language structure, language conventions (e.g., spelling and punctuation), media techniques, figurative language, and genre to create, critique, and discuss print and nonprint texts.

National TESOL Goal 3, Standard 1 (Grades 4–8): To use English in socially and culturally appropriate ways. Students will use the appropriate language variety, register, and genre according to audience, purpose, and setting.

Curriculum Standards for Life Science: Structure and function in living systems.

Materials

- Science textbook (or a handout) on the respiratory system. One possibility is *Reading Expeditions: The Human Body, The Human Machine* (National Geographic 2004b)
- Highlight pens
- Sentence strips (strips of lined tagboard)
- *Science Verse* (Scieszka 2004)
- Poster listing the essential ideas students have come to know about poetry through previous instruction

Overview

The students begin by reading *Science Verse* aloud. Scieszka discusses science concepts like the food chain, matter, and the solar system in poetic form. For example:

The Water Cycle

It's raining, it's pouring.
For H_2O, it's boring. (4)

The class discusses both the concept and the poetic form in which it was expressed. Then students write poems about human respiration.

Procedure

1. Read *Science Verse* aloud as a model for how science ideas can be conveyed in poetry.
2. Using a science text or supplementary resources, explain (in language appropriate for fifth graders) the respiratory system and how it functions.
3. Have students, in pairs, discuss their understanding of the text and explain to each other how oxygen and carbon dioxide are exchanged in the lungs.
4. Then ask each pair of students to explain the process of respiration to another pair, using drawings if necessary.
5. Once each group of four understands the text thoroughly, have each student begin to create his or her poem.
6. Have students reread the text, highlighting words or phrases that clearly communicate the function of the respiratory system.
7. Ask them to write lines on sentence strips using the underlined main ideas and important vocabulary words. (For example, "In a single day you will take 20,000 breaths of air.")
8. Have each student manipulate and sequence the lines into a poem that conveys the concept of respiration.
9. Ask students to amplify their poems by repeating pivotal words (*breathing in* and *breathing out* are good examples). Discuss what repetition does for a poem. What tone does it create?
10. Work with individual students as needed, or perhaps form groups composed of students who need particular help with reading and understanding the text, finding the vocabulary necessary to the main ideas, arranging the lines, or using repetition.
11. Again, have students, in pairs, share what they have written and revise their poems based on their partner's questions.
12. Have the students present their poems in groups of four. It is less stressful for English language learners to present to a small group rather than the entire class. Have each group choose one person to read his or her poem aloud to the whole group.

Below is an example of the type of poem students write (it doesn't have regular rhyme or rhythm, and that's okay).

Your Respiratory System

Breathe in, breathe out
20,000 breaths of air
down your trachea
to your lungs each day.

Breathe in, breathe out
Beneath your lungs
the muscle pushes.
The diaphragm moves it up.
Air leaves the lungs.

Breathe in, breathe out
Inside the lungs
millions of alveoli,
air sacs lie.
Breathe in, fresh air
called oxygen rushes
in the alveoli.

Breathe in, breathe out
Oxygen passes through alveoli
into the blood.
When done, cells let go
carbon dioxide.
Red blood cells carry
carbon dioxide back
to the alveoli.

Breathe in, breathe out
Breathe out it goes
carbon dioxide leaves your body.
It works so well
the trachea, the lungs, the alveoli to breathe.

Breathe in, breathe out
The respiratory system
How easy it is!

Assessment

Grade each student's poem based on whether or not the student explained respiration appropriately and on the use of repetition to add meaning to the poem.

Advantages for English Language Learners

Science is integrated with language arts. Many elementary schools with English language learners do not teach science because there is a laser-like focus on teaching students language arts and math. With this science lesson, there is an opportunity to manipulate language, to play with what sounds right or best by using sentence strips, and a built-in opportunity for the teacher to give individual help to students who need it.

Murals

Text can also be reframed artistically. The hieroglyphics painted on the pyramids of ancient Egypt and the primitive animal paintings found on cave walls in France are evidence that the idea of using visual images to convey meaning has been around a long time. Today's students spend huge amounts of time watching television and playing video games. A pictorial overview of ideas and concepts to be learned seems only natural and is a great way to tap into students' background experiences. Visual patterns recognized by the brain enable students to understand meaning (Farris 2004).

LESSON PLAN:
EXPLORERS/NATIVE AMERICAN MURAL

Grade Level: Fifth grade

English Language Learner Suitability: Beginning through advanced

Objective: Students will create a large mural, in colored chalk, depicting the relationship between the early explorers of America and Native Americans.

IRA/NCTE English Language Arts Standard 7: Students conduct research on issues and interests by generating ideas and questions and by posing problems. They gather, evaluate, and synthesize data from a variety of sources (e.g., print and nonprint texts, artifacts, people) to communicate their discoveries in ways that suit their purpose and audience.

National TESOL Goal 2, Standard 2: To use English to achieve academically in all content areas. Students will use English to obtain, process, construct, and provide subject matter information in spoken and written form.

Standards in History (Grades 5–12), Era 1 (Three Worlds Meet), Standard 2: How early European exploration and colonization resulted in cultural and ecological interactions among previously unconnected peoples.

Materials

- Large strips of butcher paper
- Several boxes of art chalk and rags for blending the chalk to create color shades
- Social studies textbook and/or supplementary resources
- A copy of *Encounter* (Yolen 1992)

Procedure

1. Read *Encounter* aloud. This book relates the discovery of America by Columbus from the point of view of a Taino Native American boy. It highlights perspective or point of view. (We use the book even though some critics believe that Yolen does not portray Native Americans realistically in this story. When discussing the book, we always bring up the viewpoint of those critics.)
2. Discuss point of view as it relates to the book.
3. Divide the students into groups of five: a historian, a biographer, a literary expert, an artist, and a recorder.
4. Have each group research an explorer (Hernando de Soto, Henry Hudson, Christopher Columbus, Francisco Pizarro, Magellan) using the textbook and supplementary resources. Have them answer these question.
   - Why did this explorer go to the New World?
   - What did he expect to find?
   - Did he accomplish his goals?
   - What relationship did the explorer have with Native Americans?

- How did the Native Americans relate to the explorer?
- Did these points of view change over time?

5. Ask students, as a class, to discuss the results of their inquiries and identify the main ideas.

6. Have each small group choose one idea and depict that idea visually, with the student assigned the artist role creating the sketch as the others in the group provide input. Meet with each group as they are working to make sure that each drawing depicts the ideas selected.

7. Show images of murals (use slides, books, the Internet) and ask students to describe what they see. As a class, discuss where each group's sketch will fit into a larger class mural using all of the images.

8. Have the students create the mural using colored chalk.

9. Share and post the final product. (Students can also write about what they learned in the lesson.)

Assessment

The teacher observes each group's contribution in the finished mural to see if the group portrayed a relationship between the explorers and Native Americans. If students are asked to write about what they learned through their research and painting, the teacher can look for the description and commentary of the relationship noted above.

Advantages for English Language Learners

Provide books on the topic at their reading level. Pair students who have the same primary language if they need help understanding the content or directions.

Tableaus

In Neelands and Goode's (2001) version of a tableau, students listen to or read fiction or nonfiction text and select a strategic scene to dramatize. They arrange themselves in the performing space, each student portraying a different character. Remaining motionless, each student, in turn, voices what his or her character is thinking or feeling within the context of the scene. (Each student can hold a flashlight beneath his or her chin while speaking.) Through this strategy, students begin to understand how important what a character thinks, feels, and does is to the whole story.

─────── LESSON PLAN: CIVIL WAR TABLEAU ───────

Grade Level: Eighth grade

English Language Learner Suitability: Beginning through advanced

Objective: Students reframe textbook information on the Civil War by portraying characters (real or fictional) who see the Civil War from various perspectives—Confederate and Union. Students will read about the Civil War in small groups and perform a tableau based on the perspectives of soldiers from the North and the South. They will write a summary of their performance and characterization.

IRA/NCTE English Language Arts Standard 2: Students read a wide range of literature from many periods in many genres to build an understanding of the many dimensions (e.g., philosophical, ethical, aesthetic) of human experience.

National TESOL Goal 2, Standard 2 (Grades 4–8): To use English to achieve academically in all content areas. Students will use English to obtain, process, construct, and provide subject matter information in spoken and written form.

Standards in History (Grades 5–12), Era 5 (Civil War and Reconstruction), Standard 1: The causes of the Civil War. **Standard 2:** The course and character of the Civil War and its effects on the American people.

Materials

- A social studies text
- Trade books on the Civil War:

  - *Pink and Say* (Polacco 1994), a picture book about two Union soldiers (one of them black) in Confederate territory. It portrays some of the emotional and ethical questions of war from a soldier's point of view. (For less proficient readers)
  - *Stonewall* (Fritz 1979), a chapter book biography of the military leader Stonewall Jackson that explains the war and its emotional impact on the soldiers of the North and the South. (For less proficient readers)
  - *Soldier's Heart* (Paulsen 1998), which explores the Civil War from the perspective of both soldiers and the general public. (For more proficient readers)

Procedure

1. Have small groups of students read one of the listed books.
2. Ask each group to select a strategic scene to dramatize, one that reveals how the war affected the soldiers (both North and South) who fought it.
3. Ask each group to review the scene's important ideas, events, and/or details and decide how to communicate them to the audience.
4. Have each group present its tableau, with each character telling how the war affected soldiers and talking about the physical environment of war.
5. Each student writes a summary of the effects of war on their character.

Assessment

The teacher observes the tableau and listens to the students' interpretation of the character and how the war affected the soldiers. The teacher reads the students' summaries and evaluates them in terms of characterization and the effects of war.

Advantages for English Language Learners

The other students in a group can discuss the text with English language learners and help them understand the content and the assignment. The English language learners can be given simple speeches to deliver. Beginning English language learners can draw a picture of the tableau and label it instead of writing the summary at the end.

The Chapter in a Nutshell

Scaffold: Reframing information

Teachers present information or text in an innovative way.

Appropriate grade levels: K–2, 3–5, 6–8

Strategies

Readers theatre

Miniperformance

Poetry

Murals

Tableaus

Content area

- Social studies
- Math
- Science
- Reading/language arts
- Reading
- Writing
- Listening
- Speaking
- Language processes

How is it done?

Readers theatre: Students read fiction or nonfiction text and then write and present a script that highlights the main ideas. Elaborate props or sets aren't required.

Miniperformance: Students listen to fiction or nonfiction text, create original dialogue that reveals the main ideas, make simple props, and act out the scene for an audience.

Poetry: Students read nonfiction text, talk through their understanding, write out the critical points, and manipulate these lines into poetic form.

Murals: Students read a story, talk through their understanding in small groups, decide on main points to portray using visual symbols, create a mural, and write a summary.

Tableaus: Students read or listen to text, select a scene to portray, are assigned or choose a character, and speak as that character.

Why is the scaffold important to use?

Using this scaffold improves students' reading comprehension and their confidence about reading aloud. It provides an authentic reason for English language learners to practice speaking English. Students can also understand and remember concepts longer when using this scaffold.

Developing Conversational and Academic Language

6

I
t is a puzzle to teachers and administrators alike when English language learners who have been in the American school system from kindergarten through sixth grade (or beyond) still have not reached the higher levels of English language proficiency. They seem to speak English well. They may be able to communicate with their friends, neighbors, peers, and teachers yet fail in their studies and on the standardized tests they are required to take. Here's what Sheryl, a graduate student in a teacher education program, has to say:

> As I reflected on my English language learners in the classroom and their acquisition of the English language, I thought about the judgments I had come to regarding all English language learners. I believed most of the students' language abilities were better than they actually were, based entirely

on the lack of a discernable accent when they spoke English. I never realized that one particular student, who seemed to speak English quite fluently, really didn't understand what she was learning in class. She also had a tendency to take everything said to her very literally, which created problems between her and the master teacher. . . . Another student found ways to disguise his individual lack of understanding. Ger seemed to communicate well and understand almost everything going on in the classroom. It wasn't until I really looked closely and put all the pieces together that the big picture was revealed. I have come to realize that English language learners need opportunities both formal and informal for language development, yet there are few classroom opportunities for talk.

For at least the last twenty-five years there has been an ongoing struggle over and much confusion about how best to teach English language learners. Teachers who are bilingual and have students of mostly the same language background can support their students' content understanding by teaching in the first language of the students. This is the quickest, most effective way to support content learning. Unfortunately, in most school districts in the United States the current political climate precludes teaching in the first language of the students. And for teachers who speak only English, supporting students in the first language is not even an option.

Central to the issue of teaching English language learners is a long-standing debate over whether language is acquired (Krashen and Terrel 1983) or learned (McLaughlin 1985). Each of these competing theories has had tremendous influence on knowledgeable teachers and their classroom practice.

On the one hand, some teachers refuse to teach language explicitly because they feel language should be acquired. These teachers provide frequent social interaction in their classrooms by creating opportunities for students to share information through cooperative activities in pairs, threesomes, or small groups. It is assumed that simply by being given opportunities for real collaboration, students will acquire all the language forms proficient English speakers use. But English language learners' lack of academic success points up that interaction is not enough, especially for older students.

On the other side of the debate are the teachers who favor language learning. They are likely to teach language explicitly and devote specific instruction to the fundamentals of grammar (generally out of context).

Our approach to effective language instruction for English language learners lies somewhere in between these two extremes and includes elements of both. We agree with Montano-Harmon (1999) that language instruction requires *teaching English*, not just *teaching in English* or providing opportunities for students to *interact in English*. Including student interaction in lessons and instruction is extremely valuable to English language learners: students learn a wealth of vocabulary, syntax, and ideas when they discuss their learning together. But there is more to language learning than acquisition. Older, more advanced learners of English would be more successful if their teachers taught English more explicitly.

One effective way to teach both language and content is to infuse language development throughout the content areas. This method has a number of advantages.

- ■ Students get both language and sustained content.
- ■ Students learn the academic vocabulary of each content area.
- ■ Language is kept in its natural context.
- ■ Students have reasons to use language for real purposes. (Freeman, Freeman, and Mercuri 2002)

In essence this turns all teachers into language teachers (an idea that has not gone over well with teachers mostly because they do not feel qualified to teach language in addition to their areas of expertise). But language should be taught all day long. Teachers need to plan their lessons using not only content standards but language standards as well. This way language is targeted and taught with every lesson. The lessons at the end of this chapter align with the scaffolds presented earlier but are enhanced by the addition of a language development strategy.

Knowing About Linguistics

Why is it that students can go to school for years and still not know English (or math or science or social studies)? We agree with Fillmore and Snow (2000) that part of the problem is that teachers don't understand linguistics.

As a literacy coach, Denise has spent a lot of time in many teachers' classrooms and observed first hand teachers' unfamiliarity with linguistics and grammar. Language is not being developed in a consistent and systematic manner, and English language learners remain at the beginning stages of learning English for years, if not their entire school career. Dutro and Moran (2003) maintain that linguistics needs to be taught in teacher education programs and even suggest that teachers need to be able to design a comprehensive approach to English language development.

It stands to reason that the more teachers know about how language works, the more effectively they can help their students learn. Many teachers spend huge amounts of their instructional day teaching phonics, spelling, and grammar but find that the impact on learning outcomes for English language learners is often negligible. To illustrate, over and over again teachers see that the words students misspell in their writing assignments are the very words they have studied on their spelling lists. Naturally, these teachers begin to question the value of the time spent studying spelling.

There are several reasons students don't understand language. Students may be too young or too new to English to be able to look at it in an abstract way, or the instruction does not take place in contexts in which it makes sense, or students are not given multiple opportunities in which to learn English. Some students' sole encounters with language instruction may be grammar exercises assigned as homework, without any direct instruction at all!

We need teachers to look at the full development of language—from the early stages of oral language to the most sophisticated understanding—in order to remedy this dilemma. Vygotsky (1978) established the importance of talk for all learning. Words and ideas, thoughts and language, are inseparable. It is ironic that many teachers continually ask students to be quiet in class yet wonder why their English language learners are not learning English well enough to be considered proficient and why they are so hesitant to express an idea or thought during class discussions. Research on classroom talk shows not only the importance of talk to learning but also how little talk actually occurs in classrooms (Nystrand 1997).

John Dewey once said that all learning floats on a sea of talk (Dewey 1938). In language development this is what happens—people talk to, communicate with, and relate to others as they interact in the world around them. People reflect on and share their experiences; express their needs, hopes, and fears; and in so doing learn about themselves, others, and the world in which they live. Learning and the acquisition of language are intricately connected.

Opportunities for collaboration and talk cannot be hit or miss or addressed occasionally. To that end, the TESOL English language development standards were adopted in 1997, as the role that language plays in content achievement began to be acknowledged. Many states have adopted their own language development standards as well. The TESOL standards require that a teacher consider and address the language development needs of English language learners and provide opportunities for language development in every lesson. It is important for teachers to understand that English language development, both conversational and academic, is a foundation for the understanding of content and literacy. They should not be separated.

Giving Both Conversational and Academic Language Their Due

Language can be looked at as having or not having contextual support (see Chapter 3). The amount of contextual support provided determines whether or not students can express or understand meaning. Obviously, decontextualized language is more difficult to understand, more cognitively demanding. Academic challenge is important for students' growth, but contextual support must also be present if students are to succeed academically (Cummins 1996).

Cummins (1989) defines *conversational language* as the everyday language students use for basic communication and *academic language* as the language of the classroom, which is needed for more demanding learning tasks. Gibbons (1991) has made a similar distinction between what she calls *playground language* and *classroom language*. Conversational language is developed through face-to-face interaction using gestures, visuals, and other aids that enhance understanding. This everyday conversational language is an important part of second language development because it helps children interact with their peers socially and function within the communities in which they live.

Students need to know both the language we use for speaking to one another about our daily activities and the academic language needed to be successful in school.

Academic language is decontextualized. It is the language used in textbooks, in classroom discussions, and in formal writing. It is the language used in the science book to explain the action of the ocean tides, in literature discussions on the use of metaphor, and in written reports on desert animals. Academic language requires students to use linguistic skills to access higher-level thinking. It asks students to interpret, infer, and synthesize information; to pick out the main idea; to relate ideas and information to their background experiences; to recognize the conventions of different genres; and to recognize text structure.

Students need to become proficient in academic language in order to access challenging curricula. As students move through the grades, they are asked to use language in increasingly more difficult and demanding ways. Scarcella (2001) defines *literacy* as possessing advanced levels of proficiency in the four modes of language: reading, writing, listening, and speaking. Understanding academic English allows students not only to read and understand difficult words but also to understand and use those words in spoken and written communication (10).

But academic language is more than understanding the definition of words used in content reading and discussion: that is just skimming the surface. According to Scarcella (2003), academic language plays out in:

- linguistics
- higher-order thinking skills and cognition
- society and culture

Teachers can help students develop a deeper understanding of words by planning interesting and engaging activities in which students:

- encounter words in different contexts
- are able to understand a word's meaning and use
- focus on developing ideas rather than just learning words (Freeman and Freeman 2004)

Researchers like Hoyt (2002) call the process of introducing new vocabulary and discussing concepts before reading *frontloading*. According to Hoyt, frontloading means learning about something, talking about it, wondering about it, and finally reading and writing about it. In this sense, frontloading helps students develop ideas instead of focusing on the words. It is more than a cursory look at a few words before beginning a lesson. (Chapter 4 discusses the importance of providing background knowledge and understanding.)

Academic language is defined by functions—purposes and uses—such as analyzing, comparing, predicting, persuading, synthesizing, problem solving, and evaluating (Rhodes and Solomon 1995). We say things for a reason, for social or academic purposes, in formal or informal settings. One purpose is to convey information, which includes describing people, places, and things. Another is to *create* information by making predictions or identifying causes and effects.

It is not difficult to relate a content-area language function to the standards for English language arts. Chamot and O'Malley (1987) and Lempke (1990) describe the functions of scientific language as formulating hypotheses, proposing solutions, inferring, interpreting data, and communicating findings. Short (1994) and Coehlo (1982) identify functions specific to the language of history: justifying, giving examples, sequencing, comparing and contrasting, determining causes and effects, and hypothesizing.

The *forms* of language are the tools necessary in order to carry out a function: sentence structure, parts of speech, mood, vocabulary, morphology, semantics, phonology. Here we will focus on vocabulary.

When planning vocabulary instruction and determining the words that are essential for students to know, teachers tend to focus on the terminology needed to understand specific content areas such as social studies, science, and math. In the desert web created in Chapter 4, for example, specific need-to-know words include *desert*, *nocturnal*, and *habitat*. But content-specific vocabulary like this is not the only vocabulary needed to learn about and understand the concept of *desert*.

Freeman and Freeman (2004) explain that while working on academic tasks, students encounter two types of academic vocabulary—general and content-specific—which need to be taught explicitly. Content-specific vocabulary is the vocabulary of each discipline (*photosynthesis, anarchy, plot*); general academic vocabulary includes the academic terms that appear across disciplines (*label, essay, furthermore*).

The words in the content-specific group are easy to identify. As the Freemans explain, they are usually presented in a different font in textbooks and are defined in a glossary. The general words are more difficult for all learners but especially for second language learners because they cannot be connected to any concept or theme that would make their comprehension and acquisition easier.

The following classroom vignette makes the relationship between content-specific vocabulary and general academic vocabulary a little clearer. The teacher of a fourth-grade class of mostly English language learners is teaching a lesson on the geography of California, which includes the specific words *coastal, desert,* and *mountainous*. Gina is actively involved, finding the respective regions on her map as the teacher discusses them. Clearly, she understands this specific vocabulary and is able to relate it to her map of California. But when the teacher asks the students to label the coastal region of California on their maps, Gina is brought up short. "What does *label* mean?" she asks. She is unable to show what she knows because she doesn't know what to do when cued by the essential general academic word *label*.

When choosing academic vocabulary to frontload, teachers need to consider general as well as specific vocabulary. Coxhead (2000) has created a list of academic words that are used across content areas and are important for students to master in order to be successful in accessing content and succeeding in school. These complex ideas are summarized in the concept map in Figure 6.1.

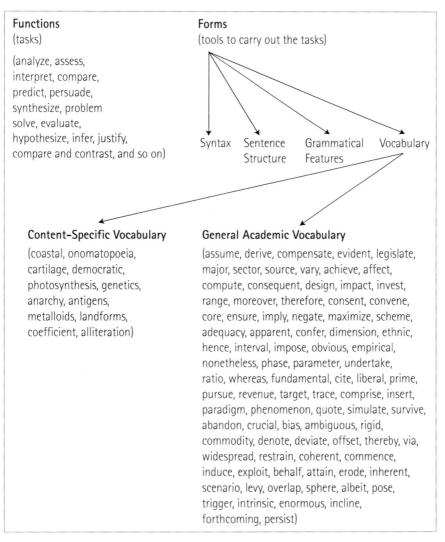

Functions
(tasks)

(analyze, assess, interpret, compare, predict, persuade, synthesize, problem solve, evaluate, hypothesize, infer, justify, compare and contrast, and so on)

Forms
(tools to carry out the tasks)

Syntax Sentence Structure Grammatical Features Vocabulary

Content-Specific Vocabulary

(coastal, onomatopoeia, cartilage, democratic, photosynthesis, genetics, anarchy, antigens, metalloids, landforms, coefficient, alliteration)

General Academic Vocabulary

(assume, derive, compensate, evident, legislate, major, sector, source, vary, achieve, affect, compute, consequent, design, impact, invest, range, moreover, therefore, consent, convene, core, ensure, imply, negate, maximize, scheme, adequacy, apparent, confer, dimension, ethnic, hence, interval, impose, obvious, empirical, nonetheless, phase, parameter, undertake, ratio, whereas, fundamental, cite, liberal, prime, pursue, revenue, target, trace, comprise, insert, paradigm, phenomenon, quote, simulate, survive, abandon, crucial, bias, ambiguous, rigid, commodity, denote, deviate, offset, thereby, via, widespread, restrain, coherent, commence, induce, exploit, behalf, attain, erode, inherent, scenario, levy, overlap, sphere, albeit, pose, trigger, intrinsic, enormous, incline, forthcoming, persist)

Figure 6.1 Academic Language

The following lessons align with the strategies presented so far, but are enhanced by combining them with a language development strategy. They address the problems previously stated.

LESSON PLAN: WEATHER

Grade Level: Kindergarten

English Language Learner Suitability: Beginning through advanced

Objective: Students will learn about the concept of weather by choosing the correct item of clothing appropriate for a rainy day, a hot day, a cold day.

IRA/NCTE English Language Arts Standard 12: Students use spoken, written, and visual language to accomplish their own purposes (e.g., for learning, enjoyment, persuasion, and the exchange of information).

National TESOL Goal 1, Standard 2: To use English to communicate in social settings. Students will interact in, through, and with spoken and written English for personal expression and enjoyment.

Curriculum Standards for Science (Grades K–4): D (Earth and Space Science), Changes in earth and sky.

Language Function

1. Conveying information—expressing needs (which articles of clothing are needed for hot, rainy, cold weather).
2. Using information—explaining (when to use a long-sleeved shirt, a jacket, a coat).

Materials

- Three plastic cartons or boxes, labeled *hot, rainy,* and *cold*
- A child's raincoat, umbrella, tank top, pair of shorts, coat, and windbreaker with a hood
- For each student, a large tagboard circle ("pizza"), one foot in diameter
- Clothing catalogs and magazines (preferably in color)
- A picture book about weather

Overview

The scaffolds in this lesson include color pictures and real items of clothing that students physically put into the appropriate boxes. The lesson also asks students to practice English by pointing to and saying academic language (the words *rainy, hot,* and *cold,* which are content-specific concepts at this age) and conversational English (the articles of clothing). (For older English language learners all these words are conversational.)

Procedure*

1. Read the picture book aloud and have a conversation about what the people on each page are wearing and why. Show the students an example of appropriate clothing for each type of weather and model how it would be worn (for example, hold up the raincoat and point out how the fabric repels water and would be good to wear in the rain).

2. Select three students to come up, one at a time, and select an article of clothing and place it in the appropriate box: hot, rainy, or cold. (They are categorizing the clothing.)

3. Have students, in small groups, choose one of the three weather conditions and then paste pictures showing that weather on one side of their individual tagboard circles.

4. The next day ask the students to cut out examples of the clothing a person would wear in that weather and paste them on the other side of the circle.

5. (*Language development strategy*) Sit in a chair facing a student and model how the students will share their circles ("pizzas"). Then ask two students to model sharing their circles with the whole group.

6. Have each student face a partner and explain the characteristics of the weather shown on one side of his or her circle. (It's fine if both partners have the same type.) Next, ask them to flip their circles over and point to and name the articles of clothing.

7. Have them repeat this sharing process with new partners as time permits.

Assessment

Circulate among the pairs of students as they describe the weather characteristics and name the related articles of clothing.

Advantages for English Language Learners

Beginning English language learners will require more time to catch on to what the lesson is about. Using visuals, modeling, and physically showing students what to do will help them. This lesson also helps English language learners because it includes real items of clothing. The students are learning the names of clothing while they are using high level learning skills to categorize. They are also learning about the concepts of what is hot, rainy and cold. It should be noted that the vocabulary of hot, rainy, and cold are considered content-specific vocabulary for this grade level of students. These are concepts for them, not just everyday language.

---

* The "pizza" strategy is adapted from Montano-Harmon 1999; we discovered the inside/outside circle strategy in Kagan 1992 and Baloche 1998.

LESSON PLAN: ALL ABOUT ME

Grade Level: Sixth grade

English Language Learner Suitability: Beginning through advanced

Objective: Students will apply an understanding of biography by writing their own auto-biographies; they will also develop their oral English vocabulary and speaking skills.

IRA/NCTE English Language Arts Standard 6: Students apply knowledge of language structure, language conventions (e.g., spelling and punctuation), media techniques, figurative language, and genre to create, critique, and discuss print and nonprint texts.

National TESOL Goal 3, Standard 1: To use English in socially and culturally appropriate ways. Students will use the appropriate language variety, register, and genre according to audience, purpose, and setting.

Language Function

1. Conveying information—describing actions, people, places, and things and retelling/relating past events.
2. Finding information—asking informational and clarifying questions.
3. Interactional—socializing by sharing personal information.

Language Form

Questioning. Explicitly teach verbs needed to talk about a person's family, pets, likes, dislikes, strengths, and favorite things. Explicitly teach verb phrases central to forming a question. Explicitly teach how questions become increasingly specific.

Materials

- For each student, a large tagboard circle ("pizza"), one foot in diameter and divided into six "slices," with five slices labeled *family*, *pets*, *likes*, *dislikes*, and *strengths*; the remaining slice will be labeled by each student to reflect one of his or her individual interests, such as *music*, *church*, *animals*, *cheerleading*, and so on.
- Pictures (preferably in color) from all kinds of magazines and/or students' personal photographs
- Colored pencils and markers
- Glue

Overview

Students learn about one another by socializing in a very structured way. With the support of peers, they preview language appropriate for an autobiography and revise their profiles to reflect their personality more accurately.

Procedure

1. Hold up the "pizza" circle, and point out the slices labeled *family, pets, likes, dislikes,* and *strengths.* Tell students they can label the remaining slice with one of their specific interests.

2. Have each student write, in abbreviated bullet points, the information to be included in each category. (For example, *family* may include brothers Samuel and Tom, sister Maria, Grandmother, Mom, and Stepdad.)

3. On the opposite side of the circle have students make a picture collage that captures who they are. (For example, a picture of Half Dome that they took on a trip to Yosemite, or a picture of Half Dome because they hope to see it someday.)

4. Let students decorate both sides of their "pizza" using colored pencils and markers. (This can be finished as homework as long as you also let them take home the materials they need.)

5. Present a minilesson or two on forms of language. How do we form questions in English? How do we form a question to get the response we intend? What verbs will we use, and how do verb phrases in questions look? Chart this information so students can refer to it as needed during the next part of the lesson.

6. Ask students to count off: one, two, one, two, one, two. Have the ones form a circle facing outward. Ask the twos to form an outer circle by standing in front of and facing a one.

7. Ask all the ones to begin talking about their "pizza." After about ninety seconds, give the twos an opportunity to ask clarifying questions they may have. (These can be as simple as "What is your dog's name?" or as complex as "Why do you want to be a musician?")

8. Have the students switch positions and roles.

9. Ask the outside row to move clockwise two or three people and then begin the discussion/questioning again. (You can do this as many times as you like and have time for.)

10. Ask the students to return to their seats and begin to write their autobiography, using their "pizza" as a prompt, perhaps writing a paragraph about each "slice."

Assessment

Look for evidence that students used information generated in the prewriting "pizza" activity in their autobiographies.

Advantages for English Language Learners

Beginning and early intermediate English language learners can complete the "pizza" and participate in the inside/outside circle (after they have previewed, with a peer, the language they will use), but they will not be able to write the autobiography.

The final lesson, for older learners, incorporates a literature study and the same strategies of "pizza" analysis and inside/outside circles. The lesson is taught after the students have completed reading *Romeo and Juliet*.

———— LESSON PLAN: *ROMEO AND JULIET* ————

Grade Level: Eighth grade

English Language Learner Suitability: Intermediate and advanced

Objective: Students will write an essay comparing and contrasting aspects of a theme in *Romeo and Juliet*.

IRA/NCTE English Language Arts Standard 1: Students read a wide range of print and nonprint texts to build an understanding of texts, of themselves, and of the cultures of the United States and the world; to acquire new information; to respond to the needs and demands of society and the workplace; and for personal fulfillment. Among these texts are fiction and nonfiction, classic and contemporary works.

National TESOL Goal 3, Standard 2 (Grades 4–8): To use English in socially and culturally appropriate ways. Students will use nonverbal communication appropriate to audience, purpose, and setting.

Language Function

1. Conveying information—describing actions, people, places, and things and retelling/relating past events.
2. Finding information—asking informational and clarifying questions.
3. Using information—expressing and supporting opinions.
4. Arranging information—compare and contrast.
5. Creating information—cause and effect, drawing conclusions, and speculating.

Language Forms

1. Present progressive tenses, adverbs (describing actions).
2. Past tenses of verbs, perfect aspect of present and past (retelling/relating past events).
3. Sentence structure, modals—*will, can, may, shall.*
4. Comparative adjectives (compare and contrast).

At this point, the teacher would stop and decide which functions and forms have already been addressed, survey the needs of the group of students, and then proceed to select a reasonable number of functions and forms to include in a lesson. The highlighted forms and functions are the ones we chose to include in this lesson.

Materials

- For each student, a large tagboard circle ("pizza"), one foot in diameter
- One completed "pizza" analysis with eight labeled slices: *character (Romeo), character (Juliet), character (Mercutio), conflict (man vs. self), conflict (man vs. man), theme (love), theme (destiny),* and *Shakespearean language*
- Scissors
- Glue
- A variety of magazines and catalogs containing pictures (preferably in color)
- Colored pencils and markers
- Copies of *Romeo and Juliet*

Procedure

1. The teacher shows the example of a completed "pizza" analysis and names the eight slices.
2. Have students complete an individual "pizza" using their own information from their unit of study.
3. Then, in successive pairings, have students share their information until everyone has a completely filled-in "pizza."
4. Have students find pictures and words related to the themes/conflicts/characters in the play and create a collage on the reverse side of the tagboard circle. (For example, one student assembled the words *family, heart, heroes, tragedy, dying, outcast, trouble, control, heart-wrenching,* and *Montague vs. Capulet.*)
5. Present minilessons on the forms of language. Review regular and irregular past tense. (Students will need the past tense to describe actions from the play.)

Introduce the present perfect and past perfect tenses if students are ready to use these tenses. Discuss the use of modals—*will, can, may, shall.*

6. Have students count off: one, two, one, two, one, two. Form an inside circle (the ones) and an outside circle (the twos).

7. In timed sessions, have pairs of students explain their "pizzas" to each other, rotating several positions clockwise between each session.

8. Have students revise their "pizzas" based on the information they gathered in the circle activity, then use them for the basis of essays comparing and contrasting aspects of either the theme of love or the theme of destiny.

Assessment

Monitor the pair discussions and the completed "pizzas" to see whether students understand the play. Formally evaluate the essays.

Advantages for English Language Learners

Adapt the language forms according to students' stages of language development. Beginning English language learners would not be expected to write an essay but could use the "pizza" to show understanding.

Final Thoughts

In conclusion, teachers must maintain a balance between providing opportunities for interaction and explicit instruction of language functions and forms. Without both, English language learners will not become competitive with native English speakers and will not become successful students.

Since many teachers have or will have at least one English language learner in their classrooms, the first step for teachers is to learn more about language. Students need to be explicitly taught through metacognitive strategies described in this book, and provided with multiple daily opportunities to use that language in meaningful and authentic ways.

In language development, people talk, communicate, and relate with others as they interact in the world around them. People reflect upon and discuss their experiences; they express their needs, hopes, and fears and in so doing, learn about themselves, others, and the world in which they live. Learning and the acquisition of language are intricately interwoven. Using the scaffolds and lesson plans provided in this book, teachers can do just that—teach and have students learn and acquire language at the same time.

Self-Assessment—Lesson Plan Chart

Appendix A

Appropriate for All Lessons, All Subject Areas

Parts of Lesson Plan		Novice Level	Apprentice Level	Proficient Level	Distinguished Level
Objective		There is no evidence that the objective is clear.	There is limited evidence that the objective is clear.	There is adequate evidence that the objective is clear.	There is strong evidence that the objective is clear.
Standards	✓ Content Standard	There is no evidence that the objective is based on standards.	There is limited evidence that the objective is based on standards.	There is adequate evidence that the objective is based on standards.	There is strong evidence that the objective is based on standards.
	✓ English Proficiency Level	There is no evidence of thought given to students' levels of English proficiency.	There is limited evidence of thought given to students' levels of English proficiency.	There is adequate evidence of thought given to students' levels of English proficiency.	There is strong evidence of thought given to students' levels of English proficiency.
Materials		There is no evidence of visuals such as pictures, photographs, videos, models, music, manipulatives, realia, computers, trade books, and props.	There is limited evidence of visuals such as pictures, photographs, videos, models, music, manipulatives, realia, computers, trade books, and props.	There is adequate evidence of visuals such as pictures, photographs, videos, models, music, manipulatives, realia, computers, trade books, and props.	There is strong evidence of visuals such as pictures, photographs, videos, models, music, manipulatives, realia, computers, trade books, and props.

Parts of Lesson Plan	Novice Level	Apprentice Level	Proficient Level	Distinguished Level
Input Strategies, Active Involvement, and Language Development: Check scaffold used. Name strategy. ___ Modeling _____ ___ Bridging _____ ___ Contextualizing _____ ___ Schema building _____ ___ Text reframing _____ ___ Language development _____	There is no evidence of support for students such as modeling, bridging, contextualizing, schema building, text representation, and/or language development. At most one strategy is present in lesson taught.	There is limited evidence of support for students such as modeling, bridging, contextualizing, schema building, text representation, and/or language development. Two strategies are present in lesson taught.	There is adequate evidence of support for students such as modeling, bridging, contextualizing, schema building, text representation, and/or language development. Three strategies are present in lesson taught.	There is strong evidence of support for students such as modeling, bridging, contextualizing, schema building, text representation, and/or language development. Four strategies are present in lesson taught.
Assessment: Check the ones used. ___ Preassess	There is no evidence that teachers can check for understanding throughout the lesson.	There is limited evidence that teachers can check for understanding throughout the lesson.	There is adequate evidence that teachers can check for understanding throughout the lesson.	There is strong evidence that teachers can check for understanding throughout the lesson.
___ Progress monitoring	There is no evidence that a wide variety of assessment methods are used.	There is limited evidence that a wide variety of assessment methods are used.	There is adequate evidence that a wide variety of assessment methods are used.	There is strong evidence that a wide variety of assessment methods are used.
___ Summative	There is no evidence that the objective is appropriate to the lesson.	There is limited evidence that the objective is appropriate to the lesson.	There is adequate evidence that the objective is appropriate to the lesson.	There is strong evidence that the objective is appropriate to the lesson.
	There is no evidence that the assessment is appropriate to students' levels of language proficiency.	There is limited evidence that the assessment is appropriate to students' levels of language proficiency.	There is adequate evidence that the assessment is appropriate to students' levels of language proficiency.	There is strong evidence that the assessment is appropriate to students' levels of language proficiency.

The Teachers and Classrooms Behind the Lesson Plans

The lesson plans were created for and used in Denise Rea's grades K–3 classes, Sandra Mercuri's grades 4–6 classes, and Ed's grades 7–8 classes. (Ed is not an actual person but a stand-in we've created to represent a composite of middle school teachers.)

Denise is a veteran teacher who began her career in southern California as a bilingual, grades K–3 elementary teacher. Her students were mostly from low-socioeconomic Spanish-speaking homes. A few English-speaking students were placed in her class as role models for the others. For several years she successfully used strategies in Spanish and English to teach her students.

Denise then moved to the central valley of California and was challenged by teaching in a school where a high percentage of students were Hmong-speaking Asians. Their families had emigrated from Laos and gravitated to this area because of the availability of farmland and agricultural work. Fifty-six percent of the students at the school had parents who did not have a high school education. Denise knew she had to reach her Hmong speakers but wasn't sure how. She began taking university classes and returned to her classroom to try each new strategy she learned. Denise learned to embed her teaching strategies in a cultural framework that connected to the students' lives, and through that modification in her instruction she was able to reach all her students.

Denise's current classroom contains twenty-three students: six English language learners at varying stages of language acquisition from beginning to almost fluent; one student on a special education individualized educational plan; two students classified as gifted and talented; and fourteen native English language speakers, three of whom are struggling in their academic work.

Sandra came to California after teaching privileged students in a private high school in Argentina. She taught grades 4–6 in a rural school in a small town in the central valley of California. Her students were diverse. In her classroom eighty percent of the students were indigenous Mexicans. Many spoke Mixteco and Triqui, languages native to southern Mexico; their Spanish skills were limited to nonexistent. All students needed to learn English and came with few literacy skills. Many of the children were members of migrant families and moved from school to school. With this challenging teaching situation, many teachers would have given up. Sandra attended university classes to gain some direction about how to teach this disparate group of students.

Sandra's class is made up of thirty students: twenty-eight students come from Spanish-speaking homes (twenty-four are beginning-to-intermediate English language learners, two speak English fluently, and two have language-processing problems), and two students are native English language speakers (one of whom also has language-processing problems).

Ed is an experienced teacher in an average-size school in a quiet neighborhood in the central valley of California. His students have been predominantly white and middle class. He works in a junior high, teaches history and English, and has between nineteen and thirty-eight students per class. The school occasionally enrolls a student who does not speak English, but they are few and far between and easily scattered throughout the classrooms. Ed avails himself of the professional development offered by his school district and prides himself on his use of instructional strategies that have allowed his students academic success. He has taught for twenty-one years and is a committed and dedicated teacher.

With the opening of a new school three years ago, the attendance boundaries changed, as did Ed's classroom composite. A new student, Harpreet, is from India. He attended school in his home country and is very knowledgeable about the grade-level content Ed teaches, although he speaks very little English. Harpreet's parents are supportive and help him understand his homework by explaining it to him in Punjabi. Another student, Maria, comes from a small town in southern Mexico. She speaks no English. Maria's parents are laborers and never had the opportunity to attend school. While Maria's parents would like her to attend school daily, she is sometimes needed at home to take care of younger siblings while her parents work.

Harpreet and Maria are by no means Ed's only new students. He has several more Hmong-speaking students as well this year. Ed continues to use the instructional strategies that have served him well in the past, but he finds that his new students are not learning English as quickly as he expected and are not scoring well on the standardized tests he is asked to administer. He finds himself at a loss as to how to proceed and hopes using scaffolds will increase his success with English language learners.

How the Lesson Plans
Are Structured

Content	• Objectives are based on national content standards and the TESOL language standards.
Connections	• There are connections to students' background knowledge. • There are connections to students' experiences and cultures. • New learning is tied to previous learning (schemas are built). • Learning strategies are explicitly taught (metacognition is developed).
Input Strategy	• Lesson strategies aid understanding. • Learning is contextualized using maps, graphic organizers, drama/role playing, props, photos (learning is active and hands on). • Lessons include demonstrations of what students are to learn (modeling).
Language Development Strategies	• There are multiple opportunities for students to engage, discuss, and question learning. • Information is reframed, and understanding is applied to these additional forms.
Assessment	• What do students already know? (Preassessment) • What do students understand and learn while the lesson is in progress? (Formative assessment) • When the lesson is over, is there evidence that students have learned what the teacher set out to teach? (Summative assessment)

Children's Literature

Bateson-Hill, M. 1998. *Shota and the Star Quilt*. Hong Kong: Anna McQuinn.

Charles, O. 1988. *How Is a Crayon Made?* New York: Scholastic.

Coerr, E. 1993. *Sadako*. New York: G. P. Putnam's Sons.

Cowley, Joy. 1999. *Red-Eyed Tree Frog*. New York: Scholastic Press.

Fox, M. 1989. *Feathers and Fools*. Singapore: Harcourt Brace & Company.

Fritz, J. 1979. *Stonewall*. New York: G. P. Putnam's Sons.

Hinton, S.E. 1967. *The Outsiders*. New York: Viking Juvenile.

Holman, S. 1999. *Grandpa, Is Everything Black Bad?* Davis, CA: The Culture CO-OP.

Hopkinson, D. 1993. *Sweet Clara and the Freedom Quilt*. New York: Alfred Knopf.

Jenkins, S. 1998. *Hottest, Coldest, Highest, Deepest*. New York: Houghton Mifflin.

Martin, Rafe. 1992. *The Rough-Face Girl*. New York: Putnam.

Mathews, P. B. 1994. *Tub Qoob Tub Loo, Farmer Boy*. Covina, CA: Pacific Asia Press.

Paulsen, Gary. 1998. *Soldier's Heart*. New York: Random House.

Polacco, P. 1994. *Pink and Say*. New York: Scholastic.

Scieszka, Jon. 2004. *Science Verse*. New York: Penguin.

Shea, D. P. 1995. *The Whispering Cloth*. Hong Kong: Boyds Mills Press.

Soto, Gary. 1995. *The Pool Party*. New York: Yearling.

Surat, M. 1983. *Angel Child, Dragon Child*. New York: Scholastic.

Tenorio-Coscarelli, J. 1996. *The Tortilla Quilt*. Hong Kong: Quarter-Inch Publishing.

Tsuchiya, Y. 1988. *Faithful Elephants: A True Story of Animals, People, and War*. New York: Houghton Mifflin.

Williams, S. 1992. *Working Cotton*. New York: Harcourt Brace Jovanovich.

Yolen, Jane. 1992. *Encounter*. New York: Harcourt Brace Jovanovich.

Bibliography

Alvermann, D., and P. Boothby. 1986. "Children's Transfer of Graphic Organizer Instruction." *Reading Psychology* 7 (2): 87–100.

Applebee, A. 1978. "Teaching High-Achievement Students: A Survey of the Winners of the 1977 NCTE Achievement Awards in Writing." *Researching in the Teaching of English*: 41–53.

Armstrong, T. 1994. *Multiple Intelligences in the Classroom.* Alexandria, VA: Association for Supervision and Curriculum Development.

Baloche, L. 1998. *The Cooperative Classroom: Empowering Learning.* Upper Saddle River, NJ: Prentice Hall.

Baloche, L, M. L. Mauger, T. M. Willis, J. R. Filinuk, and B. V. Michalsky. 1993. "Fish-bowls, Creative Controversy, Talking Chips: Exploring Literature Cooperatively." *English Journal* 82 (6): 43–48.

Bandura, A. 1986. *Social Foundations of Thought and Action: A Social Cognitive Theory.* Englewood Cliffs, NJ: Prentice Hall.

Baumann, J., L. Jones, and N. Seifert-Kessell. 1993. "Using Think-Alouds to Enhance Children's Comprehension Monitoring Abilities." *The Reading Teacher* 47 (3): 184–93.

Bearse, C., and J. Harutunian. 2005. "Writing for English Language Learners." Paper presented at the National Association for Bilingual Education, San Antonio, TX.

Benson, P. 2002. *How to Meet the Standards, Motivate Students, and Still Enjoy Teaching: Four Practices That Improve Student Learning.* Thousand Oaks, CA: Corwin.

Block, C. C. 2003. *Teaching Comprehension: The Comprehension Process Approach.* Boston: Allyn and Bacon.

Block, C. C., and S. E. Israel. 2004. "The ABCs of Performing Highly Effective Think-Alouds: Effective Think-Alouds Can Build Students' Comprehension, Decoding, Vocabulary, and Fluency." *The Reading Teacher* 58 (2): 154–57.

Bloom, B. S., ed. 1956. *Taxonomy of Educational Objectives: The Classification of Educational Goals.* Handbook I: Cognitive Domain. New York: Longman; Toronto: Green.

Brandt, R. 1990. "On Cooperative Learning: A Conversation with Spencer Kagan." *Educational Leadership* 47 (4): 8–11.

California State Department of Education. 1996. Retrieved August 2, 2004, from www.cde.ca.gov.

Chamot, A., and J. O'Malley. 1987. "The Cognitive Academic Language Learning Approach: A Bridge to the Mainstream." *TESOL Quarterly* 21: 227–49.

Coehlo, E. 1982. "Language Across the Curriculum." *TESOL Talk* 13: 56–70.

Coffey, J. W., M. J. Carnot, P. J. Feltovich, J. L. Feltovich, R. R. Hoffman, A. J. Canas et al. 2003. *A Summary of Literature Pertaining to the Use of Concept Mapping Techniques and Technologies for Education and Performance Support*. Technical Report submitted to the U.S. Navy Chief of Naval Education and Training. Pensacola, FL: Institute for Human and Machine Cognition.

Cohen, E. 2003. "Complex Instruction Who's Who." Retrieved April 4, 2003, from http://cgi.stanford.edu/group/pci/cgi-bin/site.cgi?page=whos_who.html.

Cohen, E., and R. Lotan. 1997. *Working for Equity in Heterogeneous Classrooms: Sociological Theory in Practice*. New York: Teachers College Press.

Commander, N. E., and M. Valeri-Gold. 2001. "The Learning Portfolio: A Valuable Tool for Increasing Metacognitive Awareness." *The Learning Assistance Review* 6 (2): 5–18.

Copeland, R. 1974. *How Children Learn Mathematics: Teaching Implications of Piaget's Research*. New York: Macmillan.

Corson, D. 1995. *Using English Words*. New York: Kluwer.

Coxhead, A. 2000. "A New Academic Word List." *TESOL Quarterly* 2: 213–38.

Crawford, L. 1993. *Language and Literacy Learning in Multicultural Classrooms*. Needham Heights, MA: Allyn and Bacon.

Cummins, J. 1996. "Negotiating Identities: Education for Empowerment in a Diverse Society." Covina: California Association for Bilingual Education.

———. 1989. "Empowering Minority Students." Covina: California Association for Bilingual Education.

———. 1981. "Bilingualism and Minority Language Children." Toronto: Ministry of Education.

Cunningham, A., and R. Shagoury. 2005. *Starting with Comprehension: Reading Strategies for the Youngest of Learners*. Portland, ME: Stenhouse.

Cunningham, P. M., S. A. Moore, J. W. Cunningham, and D. W. Moore. 1995. *Reading and Writing in Elementary Classrooms: Strategies and Observations*, 3d ed. New York: Longman.

DeLisi, R. 2002. "From Marbles to Instant Messenger? The Implications of Piaget's Ideas About Peer Learning." *Theory into Practice* 41 (1): 5–12.

Dewey, J. 1938. *Experience and Education*. New York: Macmillan.

Dutro, S., and C. Moran. 2003. "Rethinking English Language Instruction: An Architectural Approach." In *English Learners: Reaching the Highest Level of English Literacy,* ed. G. Garcia. Upper Saddle River, NJ: Pearson.

Farris, P. J. 2004. *Elementary and Middle School Social Studies: An Interdisciplinary and Multicultural Approach*, 4th ed. Boston: McGraw-Hill.

Feuerstein, R. 1980. *Instrumental Enrichment: An Intervention Program for Cognitive Modifiability*. Baltimore: University Park Press.

Fillmore, L. W., and C. Snow. 2000. "What Teachers Need to Know About Language." *ERIC Clearinghouse on Languages and Linguistics and Linguistics Online.*

Fogarty, R., 1999. "Architects of the Intellect." *Educational Leadership* 57 (3): 76–78.

Freeman, D. E., and Y. S. Freeman. 2005. *Essential Linguistics: What You Need to Know to Teach Reading, ESL, Spelling, Phonics, and Grammar*. Portsmouth, NH: Heinemann.

———. 2001. *Between Worlds: Access to Second Language Acquisition.* Portsmouth, NH: Heinemann.

Freeman, Y. S., and D. E. Freeman. 2004. "Preview, View, Review: Giving Multilingual Learners Access to the Curriculum." In *Spotlight on Comprehension: Building a Literacy of Thoughtfulness*, ed. L. Hoyt. Portsmouth, NH: Heinemann.

———. 1998. *ESL/EFL Teaching: Principles for Success*. Portsmouth, NH: Heinemann.

Freeman, Y. S, D. E. Freeman, and S. Mercuri. 2002. *Closing the Achievement Gap: How to Reach Limited-Formal-Schooling and Long-Term English Learners*. Portsmouth, NH: Heinemann.

Garcia, G. E. 2002. "Issues Surrounding Cross-Linguistic Transfer in Bilingual Students' Reading: A Study of Mexican-American Fourth Graders." Paper presented at the National Reading Conference, Miami, FL, December.

Gardner, H. 1999. *Intelligence Reframed: Multiple Intelligences for the 21st Century*. New York: Basic Books.

———. 1983. *Frames of Mind: The Theory of Multiple Intelligences*. New York: Basic Books.

Gibbons, P. 1991. *Learning to Learn in a Second Language*. Portsmouth, NH: Heinemann.

Griffin, C., and B. Tulbert. 1995. "The Effect of Graphic Organizers on Students' Comprehension and Recall of Expository Text: A Review of the Research and Implications for Practice." *Reading and Writing Quarterly: Overcoming Learning Difficulties* 11 (1): 73–89.

Grinder, M. 1995. *Envoy: Your Personal Guide to Classroom Management*. Battleground, WA: MGA Publishing Consortium.

Halliday, M. 1973. *Explorations in the Functions of Language*. London: Edward Arnold.

Hibbing, A. N., and J. L. Rankin-Erickson. 2003. "A Picture Is Worth a Thousand Words: Using Visual Images to Improve Comprehension for Middle School Struggling Readers." *The Reading Teacher* 56 (8): 758–70.

Hoyt, L. 2002. *Make It Real: Strategies for Success with Informational Texts*. Portsmouth, NH: Heinemann.

Israel, S. E. 2002. Understanding Strategy Utilization During Reading Comprehension: Relations Between Text Type and Reading Levels Using Verbal Protocols. Unpublished doctoral dissertation, Teachers College, Ball State University, Muncie, IN.

Jaramillo, J. 1996. "Vygotsky's Sociocultural Theory and Contributions to the Development of Constructivist Curricula." *Education* 117 (11): 133–40.

Jensen, E. 1998. *Teaching with the Brain in Mind*. Alexandria, VA: Association for Supervision and Curriculum Development.

Kagan, S. 1994. *Cooperative Learning*. San Clemente, CA: Kagan Cooperative Learning.

———. 1992. *Cooperative Learning*. San Juan Capistrano, CA: Kagan Cooperative Learning.

———. 1990. *Cooperative Learning Resources for Teachers*. San Juan Capistrano, CA: Resources for Teachers.

Krashen, S. 1985. *The Input Hypothesis: Issues and Implications*. New York: Longman.

Krashen, S., and T. Terrel. 1983. *The Natural Approach: Language Acquisition in the Classroom*. San Francisco: Alemany Press.

Lakoff, G., and M. Johnson. 1980. *Metaphors We Live By*. Chicago: University of Chicago Press.

Lempke, J. 1990. *Talking Science: Language, Learning, and Values.* New York: Ablex.

McCaslin, N. 1990. *Creative Drama in the Classroom*. New York: Longman.

McKenzie, J. 2000. *Scaffolding for Success: Beyond Technology, Questioning, Research and the Information Literate School Community.* Electronic version. Retrieved November 21, 2004, from http://fno.org/dec99/scaffold.html.

McLaughlin, B. 1985. *Second-Language Acquisition in Childhood: School-Age Children*. Hillsdale, NJ: Erlbaum.

Meyer, B. J., and R. O. Freedle. 1984. "Effects of Discourse Type on Recall." *American Educational Research Journal* 21: 121–43.

Miller, D. 2002. *Reading with Meaning: Teaching Comprehension in the Primary Grades*. Portland, ME: Stenhouse.

Montano-Harmon, M. 1999. "Developing English for Academic Purposes." Paper presented at the EAP Summer Institute, Fullerton, CA.

Morado, C., R. Koenig, and A. Wilson. 1999. "Miniperformances, Many Stars! Playing with Stories." *The Reading Teacher* 53 (2): 116–23.

National Geographic. 2004a. *Reading Expeditions: Earth Science, The Oceans Around Us*. Washington, DC: National Geographic Society.

———. 2004b. *Reading Expeditions: The Human Body, The Human Machine*. Washington, DC: National Geographic Society.

———. 2004c. *Reading Expeditions, Earth Science, Rocks and Minerals*. Washington, DC: National Geographic Society.

———. 2004d. *Reading Expeditions, Nonfiction Reading and Writing Workshops, Articles Using Sequence*. Washington, DC: National Geographic Society.

Neelands, J., and T. Goode. 2001. *Structuring Drama Work: A Handbook of Available Forms in Theatre and Drama*. Cambridge, UK: Cambridge University Press.

Novak, J. 2002. "Meaningful Learning: The Essential Factor for Conceptual Change in Limited or Inappropriate Propositional Hierarchies Leading to Empowerment of Learners." *Science Education* 16 (4): 548–71.

Novak, J. D., and D. B. Gowin. 1984. *Learning How to Learn*. New York: Cambridge University Press.

Nystrand, M. 1997. *Opening Dialogue: Understanding the Dynamics of Language and Learning in the English Classroom*. New York: Teachers College Press.

Olsen, L. 1988. *Immigrant Youth in California Public Schools: Crossing the Schoolhouse Border*. San Francisco: California Tomorrow.

Oster, L. 2001. "Using the Think Aloud for Reading Instruction." *The Reading Teacher* 55: 65–69.

Piaget, J. 1970. *The Science of Education and the Psychology of the Child*. New York: Grossman.

Polloway, E., J. Patton, and L. Serna. 2001. *Strategies for Teaching Learners with Special Needs*, 7th ed. Upper Saddle River, NJ: Prentice Hall.

Pressley, M., and P. Afflerbach. 1995. *Verbal Protocols of Reading: The Nature of Constructively Responsive Reading*. Hillsdale, NJ: Erlbaum.

Rhodes, N., and J. Solomon. 1995. "Conceptualizing Academic Language." Research Report Paper 15. Santa Cruz, CA: Center for Research on Education, Diversity, and Excellence.

Robb, L. 2003. *Teaching Reading in Social Studies, Science, and Math*. New York: Scholastic.

Rosenshine, B. 1997. "Advances in Research on Instruction." In *Issues in Educating Students with Disabilities*, ed. J. W. Lloyd, E. J. Kameanui, and D. Chard, 197–221. Mahwah, NJ: Erlbaum.

Rumelhart, D. E. 1980. "Schemata: The Building Blocks of Cognition." In *Theoretical Issues in Reading Comprehension*, ed. Rand J. Spiro et al., 33–58. Hillsdale, NJ: Erlbaum.

Samuels, S. J. 1997. "The Method of Repeated Readings." *The Reading Teacher* 50: 76–81.

Sanders, W., and J. Rivers. 1996. *Cumulative and Residual Effects of Teachers on Future Student Academic Achievement.* Research Progress Report. Knoxville: University of Tennessee Value Added Research and Assessment Center.

Scarcella, R. 2003. *Academic English: A Conceptual Framework*. Technical Report 2003-1. Irvine: University of California Linguistic Minority Research Institute.

———. 2001. "Effective Writing Instruction for English Language Learners: California English."

Shepard, A. 2004. "Aaron Shepard's RT page." Retrieved December 2004, from www.aaronshep.com.

Short, D. 1994. "Expanding Middle School Horizons: Integrating Language, Culture, and Social Studies." *TESOL Quarterly* 28: 581–608.

Skutnabb-Kangas, T. 1981. *Bilingualism or Not: The Education of Minorities*. Translated by L. Malmberg and D. Crane. Clevendon, England: Multilingual Matters.

Smith, P. L., and G. E. Tompkins. 1988. "Structured Notetaking: A Strategy for Content Area Readers." *Journal of Reading* 32: 46–53.

Snow, C., H. Cancino, J. de Temple, and S. Schley. 1991. "Giving Formal Definitions: A Linguistic or Metalinguistic Skill?" In *Language Processing in Bilingual Children*, 90–112. New York: New York University Press.

Sousa, D. 2000. *How the Brain Learns*. Reston, VA: National Association of Secondary School Principals.

Swain, M. 1985. "Communicative Competence: Some Roles of Comprehensible Input and Comprehensible Output in Its Development." In *Input in Second Language Acquisition*, ed. C. Madden and S. Gass, 235–53. Rowley, MA: Newbury House.

Tomlinson, C. A. 2003. *Fulfilling the Promise of the Differentiated Classroom: Strategies and Tools for Responsive Teaching.* Alexandria, VA: Association for Supervision and Curriculum Development.

Vacca, R. T., and J. L. Vacca. 1999. *Content Area Reading: Literacy and Learning Across the Curriculum*, 6th ed. New York: Longman.

Vygotsky, L. S. 1978. *Mind in Society: The Development of Higher Psychological Processes*. Cambridge, MA: Harvard University Press.

Walqui van Lier, A. 2003. *A Conceptual Framework for Scaffolding Instruction for English Learners*. San Francisco: WestEd.

Weimer, M. 2002. *Five Key Changes to Practice*. San Francisco: Jossey-Bass.

Westwater, A., and P. Wolfe. 2000. "The Brain Compatible Curriculum." *Educational Leadership* 11: 49–52.

Wiggins, G., and J. McTighe. 1998. *Understanding by Design*. New York: Merrill Prentice Hall.

Wilhelm, J. 2001. *Improving Comprehension with Think-Aloud Strategies*. New York: Scholastic.

Worthy, J., and K. Prater. 2002. "I Thought About It All Night: Readers Theatre for Reading Fluency and Motivation." *The Reading Teacher* 56 (3): 294–97.

Index